Collins Primary World Atlas

Globes and maps

Globes are models of the earth. The seven global views below show the true shape and size of the continents.

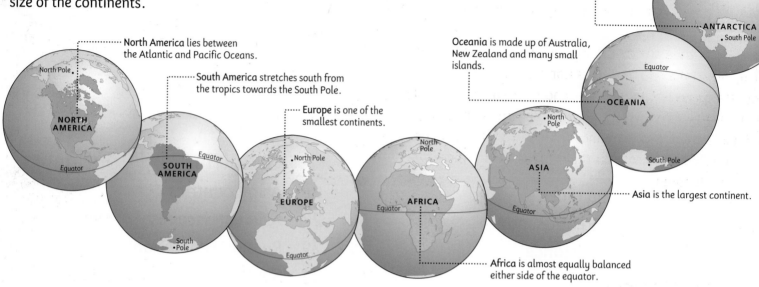

Antarctica encircles the South Pole.

North America lies between the Atlantic and Pacific Oceans.

South America stretches south from the tropics towards the South Pole.

Europe is one of the smallest continents.

Oceania is made up of Australia, New Zealand and many small islands.

Asia is the largest continent.

Africa is almost equally balanced either side of the equator.

Mapping the world

To show the world on a flat map we need to peel the surface of the globe and flatten it out. There are many different methods of altering the shape of the earth so that it can be mapped on an atlas page. These methods are called **projections**.

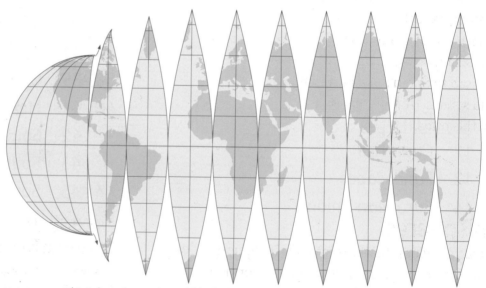

This is how the earth would look if the surface could be peeled and laid flat.

Projections

Map projections change the shape and size of the continents and oceans. The projection used for world maps in this atlas is called Eckert IV.

How the world map looks, depends on which continents are at the centre of the map. Compare the shape of Africa on the maps below to that on the globe.

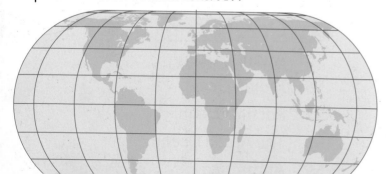

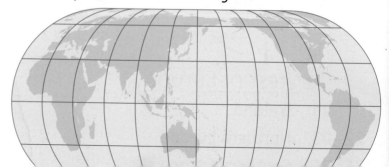

Latitude and longitude

Every feature in the world can be located accurately. We use latitude and longitude to locate where features are. Latitude and longitude form our global positioning system.

Lines of latitude are imaginary lines which circle the earth. They are numbered in degrees North or South of the equator. Lines of longitude are imaginary lines which run from the North to the South Poles. They are numbered in degrees East or West of a line through London known as the Prime Meridian. We use the degrees to say where any feature is located.

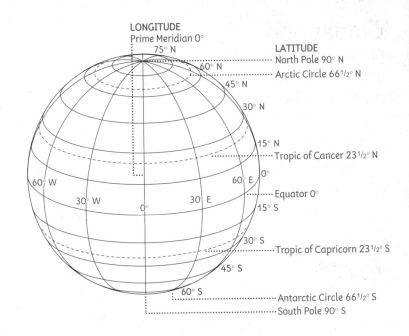

Grid references

Lines of latitude and longitude are used in this atlas to make a grid. By labelling the columns in the grid with a letter and the rows with a number a simple grid code e.g. B6 can be used to find all places within one grid square. This system is used in this atlas.

Cartagena is in B8

Bogotá is in B7

Piura is in A6

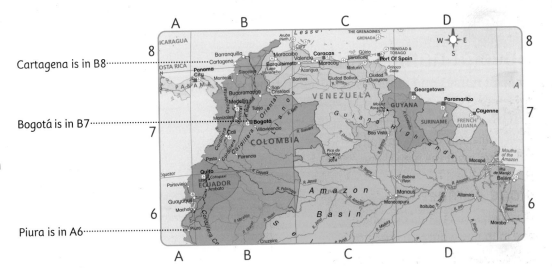

Hemispheres

The equator divides the globe into two imaginary halves. All land north of the equator is called the northern hemisphere. Land south of the equator is called the southern hemisphere. 0° and 180° lines of longitude also divide the globes into two imaginary halves, the western and eastern hemispheres.

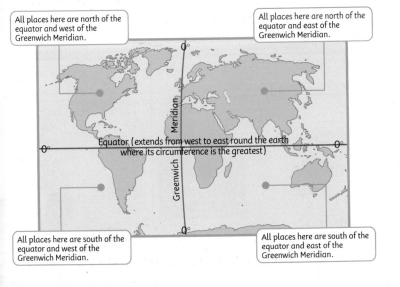

All places here are north of the equator and west of the Greenwich Meridian.

All places here are north of the equator and east of the Greenwich Meridian.

All places here are south of the equator and west of the Greenwich Meridian.

All places here are south of the equator and east of the Greenwich Meridian.

Direction

On most atlas maps you will find a compass. It names the four compass points North (N), East (E), South (S) and West (W). Between each main point are intermediate points Northeast, Southeast, Southwest and Northwest. These help us give more accurate directions.

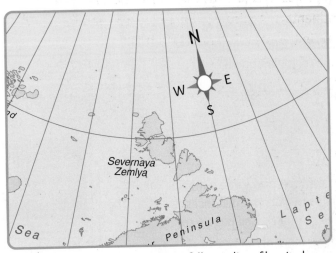

On atlas maps the north point always follows a line of longitude

Atlas maps

Atlas maps tell us about the various parts of the world. They tell us about different environments in the world.

Some maps show country shapes and where towns are located within the country. These are called political maps.

Some maps show landscapes. They show the physical environment.

Special names and numbers

Special names and numbers are used to label parts of an atlas map.

Title
This names the map area and describes what the map shows.

Page number
This helps you to find out where the map you want is in the atlas.

Locator map
This shows the part of the world covered by the map.

Area comparison
This map shows the size of the British Isles compared to the region mapped.

Scale
This explains how large a map is. It helps to work out distances between places. See page 6 to find out more about scale.

Compass
This always points north-south on the map. It shows east and west. Other directions can be found from the compass.

Key
This explains what the colours and symbols used on the map represent.

Fact boxes
These contain interesting information about a continent.

Map symbols

Maps are made up of symbols and names. The symbols can be points, lines or area colours. A map is complete when the symbols and the names are combined.

Point symbols

- Town stamps
- Mountain peaks
- Airports

Lines

- —— Roads
- ----- Railways
- —— Rivers and canals
- —— Coastline

Area colours

- Lake/sea
- Country colours

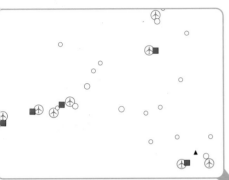

Point symbols are used on a map to show towns, mountain peaks and airports.

Lines are used an a map to show communications and drainage.

Area colours are used to distinguish one country from another and the land from the sea.

Names on atlas maps

The style and size of the type used on maps helps to explain what the name means.

Large bodies of water

PACIFIC OCEAN

Gulf of Guinea

Islands

Cuba

Bioco

Countries

NIGERIA

BENIN

Large cities

Porto-Novo

Lomé

Small towns

Parakou

Enugu

Rivers

Mississippi

Nile

Amazon

Mountain peaks

Mount Cameroon

Everest

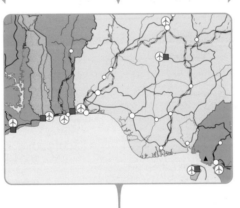

All the symbols are combined to show features and their correct locations.

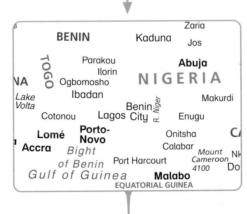

Names are needed to show places and features shown on the map. Only some places and features are named.

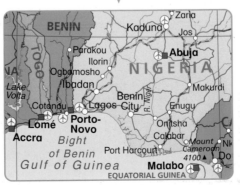

The map is complete when the symbols and the names are combined.

Scale

Maps are much smaller than the regions they show. To
compare the real area with the mapped area you have
to use a scale. Each map in this atlas shows its scale.
This is shown using a scale bar which is explained in words.

E.g. 0   200   400   600   800 km

Scale : One centimetre on this map is the same as 200 kilometres on the ground.

Large scale maps
show smaller areas
with more detail.

LARGE SCALE

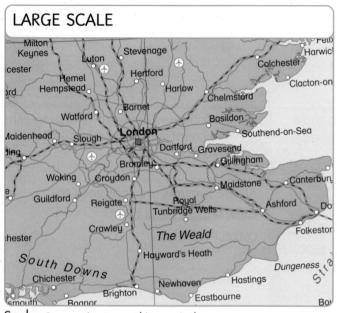

Scale: One centimetre on this map is the same as
20 kilometres on the ground.

0   20   40   60   80   100 km

MEDIUM SCALE

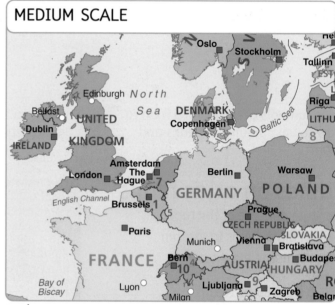

Scale: One centimetre on this map is the same as
250 kilometres on the ground.

0   250   500   750   1000   1250 km

Measuring distance

The scale of a map can be used to measure how far it is
between two places. For example, the straight line distance
between Boa Vista and Cayenne on the map to the right is
5 centimetres.

Look at the ruler.
One centimetre on this map is the same as 200 kilometres on
the ground. The real distance between Boa Vista and Cayenne
is therefore 1000 kilometres (i.e. 5 X 200).

0   200   400   600   800 km

Scale : One centimetre on thi

Extend your knowledge and understanding by visiting these websites which provide lots of information and material to help with your homework and projects.

British Isles

Places to visit
Visit Britain www.visitbritain.com
Tourism in Ireland www.tourismireland.com
www.discoverireland.ie

Weather and climate
The Met Office www.metoffice.gov.uk
BBC weather www.bbc.co.uk/weather

Landscapes and rivers
Learning through landscapes www.ltl.org.uk
Learning rivers www.swgfl.org.uk/rivers

Scottish landscapes
www.bbc.co.uk/scotland/education/sysm/landscapes

Statistics
National statistics www.statistics.gov.uk/glance

Europe
European Union www.europa.eu.int/abc/index_en.htm

World

Climate
World climate statistics www.worldclimate.com

Population
City populations www.citypopulation.de

Geography
Royal Geographical Society www.rgs.org
National Geographic www.nationalgeographic.com

Mountains
Mountains of the world www.peakware.com

Satellite images
Earth Observatory earthobservatory.nasa.gov
Visible Earth visibleearth.nasa.gov
MODIS satellite images modis.gsfc.nasa.gov

Development issues
Global Eye www.globaleye.org.uk

Flags
Flags of the world www.theodora.com/flags

International organisations
ActionAid International www.actionaid.org
The Commonwealth www.youngcommonwealth.org
Christian Aid www.globalgang.org.uk
United Nations www.cyberschoolbus.un.org

Small scale maps show larger areas with less detail.

SMALL SCALE

Scale: One centimetre on this map is the same as 800 kilometres on the ground.

0   800   1600   2400   3200 km

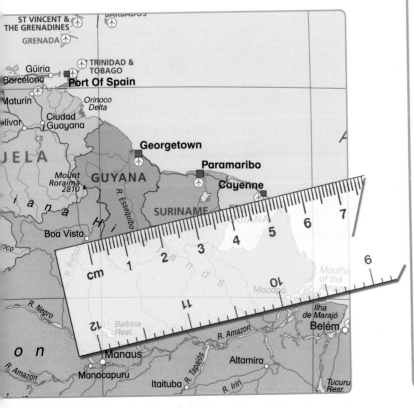

he same as 200 kilometres on the ground.

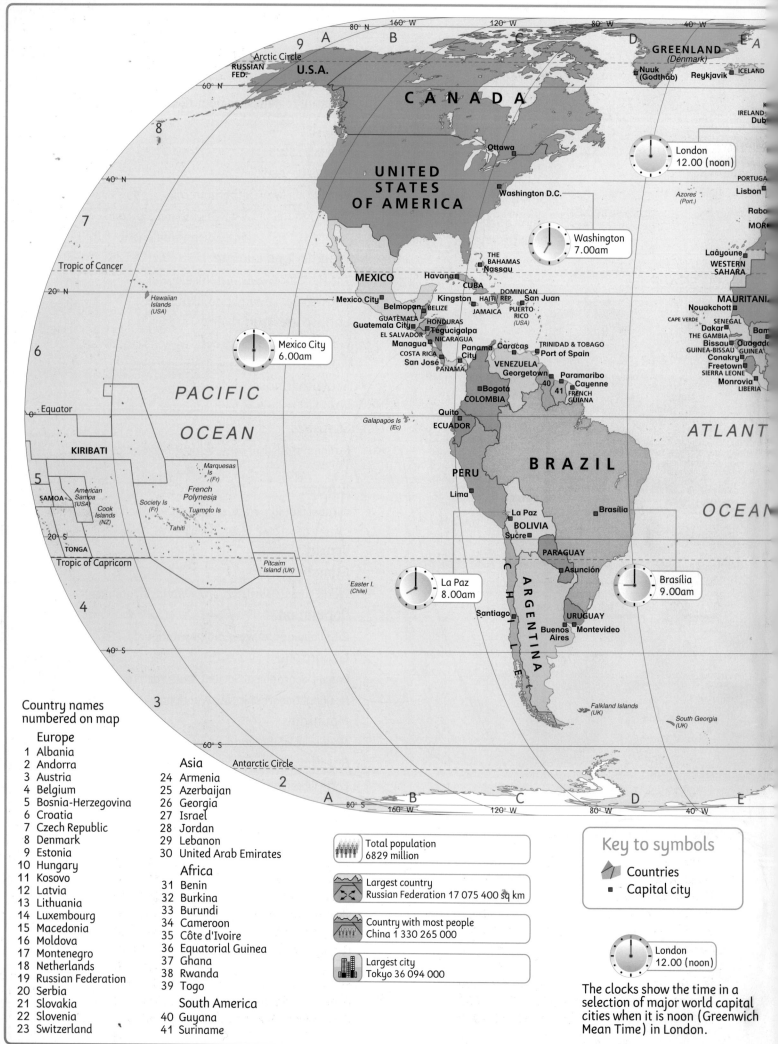

Arctic Circle

RUSSIAN FED.

U.S.A.

GREENLAND (Denmark)

Nuuk (Godthåb) Reykjavik ICELAND

C A N A D A

IRELAND Dub

London 12.00 (noon)

UNITED STATES OF AMERICA

Ottawa

Washington D.C.

PORTUGA

Lisbon

Azores (Port.)

Rabo

MOR

Washington 7.00am

Tropic of Cancer

MEXICO

THE BAHAMAS

Havana Nassau

CUBA

Laâyoune

WESTERN SAHARA

MAURITANI

Hawaiian Islands (USA)

Mexico City

Belmopan BELIZE

Kingston HAITI REP. San Juan

JAMAICA PUERTO RICO (USA)

DOMINICAN

Nouakchott

CAPE VERDE SENEGAL

Dakar

GUATEMALA HONDURAS

Guatemala City

EL SALVADOR Tegucigalpa

Managua NICARAGUA

COSTA RICA

San José PANAMA

Panama City

Caracas

TRINIDAD & TOBAGO

Port of Spain

VENEZUELA

Georgetown Paramaribo

40 41 Cayenne

FRENCH GUIANA

THE GAMBIA Bam

Bissau Ouagado

GUINEA-BISSAU GUINEA

Conakry

Freetown

SIERRA LEONE

Monrovia

LIBERIA

Mexico City 6.00am

PACIFIC

OCEAN

Equator

Galapagos Is (Ec)

Bogotá

COLOMBIA

Quito

ECUADOR

ATLANT

KIRIBATI

Marquesas Is (Fr)

French Polynesia

PERU

Lima

B R A Z I L

OCEAN

SAMOA

American Samoa (USA)

Society Is (Fr)

Cook Islands (NZ)

Tuamoto Is

Tahiti

La Paz

BOLIVIA

Sucre

Brasília

TONGA

Tropic of Capricorn

Pitcairn Island (UK)

Easter I. (Chile)

La Paz 8.00am

PARAGUAY

Asunción

Brasília 9.00am

A R G E N T I N A

C H I L E

Santiago

URUGUAY

Buenos Aires Montevideo

Falkland Islands (UK)

South Georgia (UK)

Antarctic Circle

Country names numbered on map

Europe

1 Albania
2 Andorra
3 Austria
4 Belgium
5 Bosnia-Herzegovina
6 Croatia
7 Czech Republic
8 Denmark
9 Estonia
10 Hungary
11 Kosovo
12 Latvia
13 Lithuania
14 Luxembourg
15 Macedonia
16 Moldova
17 Montenegro
18 Netherlands
19 Russian Federation
20 Serbia
21 Slovakia
22 Slovenia
23 Switzerland

Asia

24 Armenia
25 Azerbaijan
26 Georgia
27 Israel
28 Jordan
29 Lebanon
30 United Arab Emirates

Africa

31 Benin
32 Burkina
33 Burundi
34 Cameroon
35 Côte d'Ivoire
36 Equatorial Guinea
37 Ghana
38 Rwanda
39 Togo

South America

40 Guyana
41 Suriname

Total population 6829 million

Largest country Russian Federation 17 075 400 sq km

Country with most people China 1 330 265 000

Largest city Tokyo 36 094 000

Key to symbols

Countries

Capital city

London 12.00 (noon)

The clocks show the time in a selection of major world capital cities when it is noon (Greenwich Mean Time) in London.

0 800 1600 2400 3200 km

Scale : One centimetre on this map is the same as 800 kilometres on the ground.

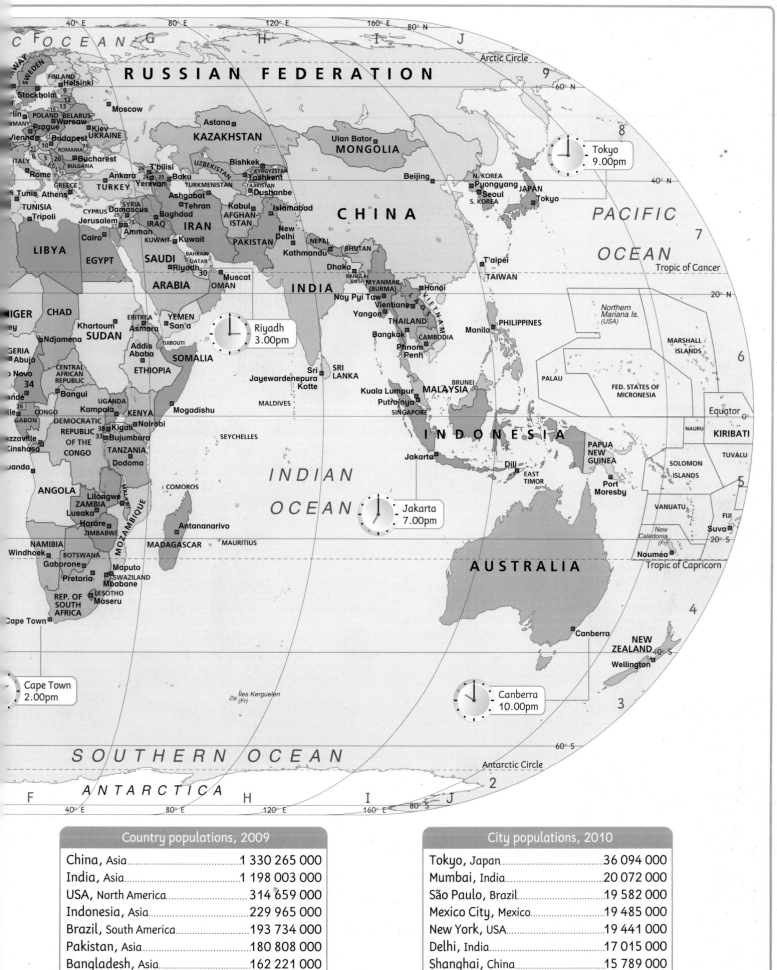

Country populations, 2009	
China, Asia	1 330 265 000
India, Asia	1 198 003 000
USA, North America	314 659 000
Indonesia, Asia	229 965 000
Brazil, South America	193 734 000
Pakistan, Asia	180 808 000
Bangladesh, Asia	162 221 000
Nigeria, Africa	154 729 000
Russian Federation, Asia/Europe	140 874 000
Japan, Asia	127 156 000

City populations, 2010	
Tokyo, Japan	36 094 000
Mumbai, India	20 072 000
São Paulo, Brazil	19 582 000
Mexico City, Mexico	19 485 000
New York, USA	19 441 000
Delhi, India	17 015 000
Shanghai, China	15 789 000
Kolkata, India	15 577 000
Dhaka, Bangladesh	14 796 000
Buenos Aires, Argentina	13 089 000

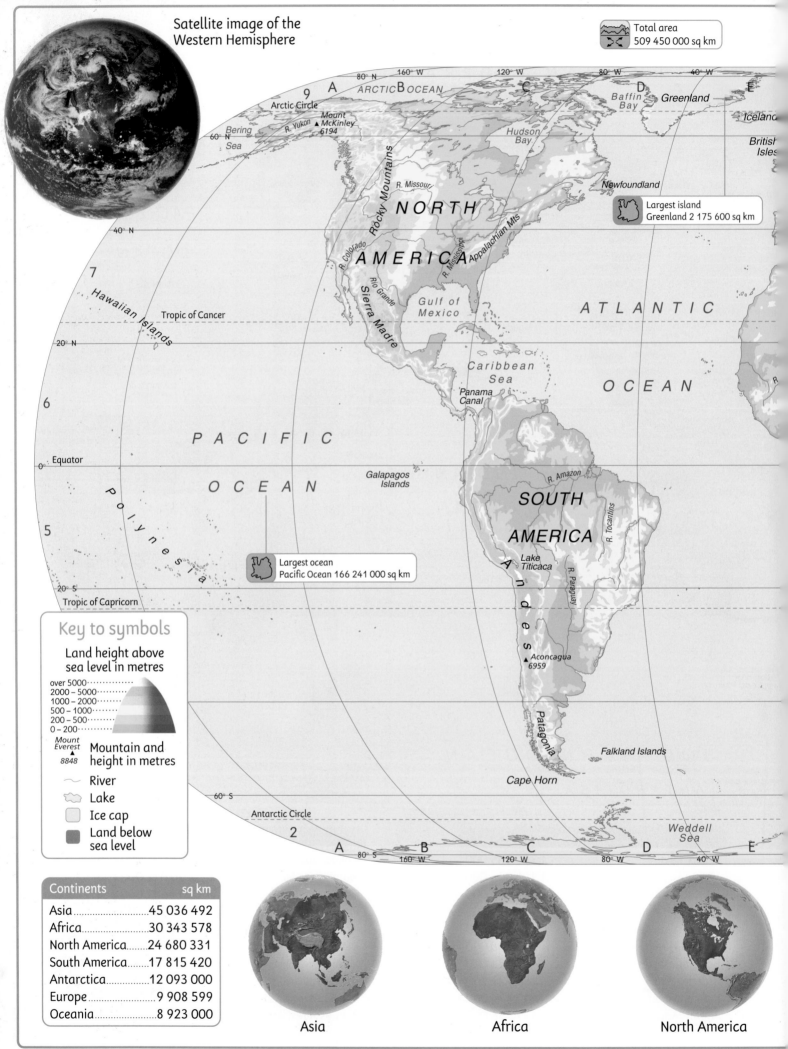

Satellite image of the Western Hemisphere

Total area
509 450 000 sq km

Largest island
Greenland 2 175 600 sq km

Largest ocean
Pacific Ocean 166 241 000 sq km

ARCTIC OCEAN

Arctic Circle

Bering Sea

R. Yukon Mount McKinley 6194

Rocky Mountains

R. Missouri

NORTH

AMERICA

R. Colorado

Sierra Madre

Rio Grande

Tropic of Cancer

Hawaiian Islands

Gulf of Mexico

R. Mississippi

Appalachian Mts

Baffin Bay Greenland

Iceland

British Isles

Hudson Bay

Newfoundland

ATLANTIC

OCEAN

Caribbean Sea

Panama Canal

PACIFIC

OCEAN

Polynesia

Equator

Galapagos Islands

SOUTH

AMERICA

R. Amazon

R. Tocantins

Lake Titicaca

R. Paraguay

Andes

Tropic of Capricorn

Aconcagua 6959

Patagonia

Falkland Islands

Cape Horn

Weddell Sea

Antarctic Circle

Key to symbols

Land height above sea level in metres

over 5000
2000 – 5000
1000 – 2000
500 – 1000
200 – 500
0 – 200

Mount Everest ▲ 8848 Mountain and height in metres

River

Lake

Ice cap

Land below sea level

Continents	sq km
Asia	45 036 492
Africa	30 343 578
North America	24 680 331
South America	17 815 420
Antarctica	12 093 000
Europe	9 908 599
Oceania	8 923 000

Asia   Africa   North America

0   800   1600   2400   3200 km

Scale : One centimetre on this map is the same as 800 kilometres on the ground.

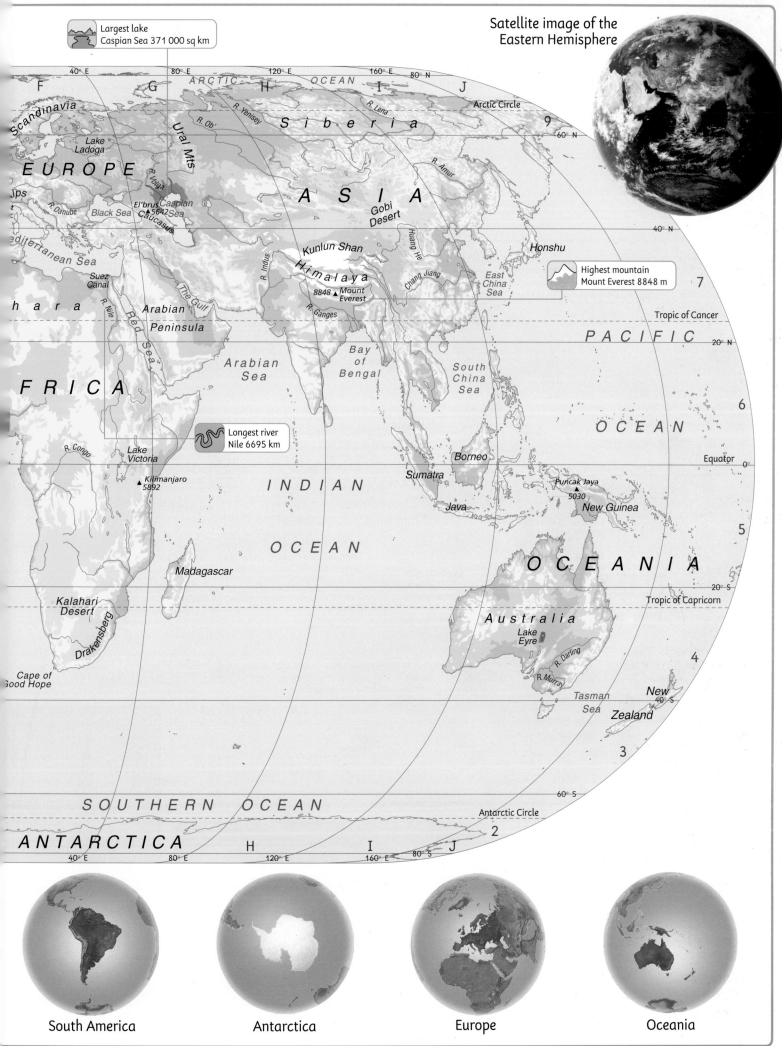

Largest lake
Caspian Sea 371 000 sq km

Satellite image of the
Eastern Hemisphere

Highest mountain
Mount Everest 8848 m

Longest river
Nile 6695 km

ARCTIC OCEAN

Scandinavia

R. Yenisey
R. Ob'
R. Lena

S i b e r i a

Arctic Circle

Lake
Ladoga

Ural Mts

EUROPE

R. Volga

A S I A

R. Amur

lps

R. Danube

El'brus Caspian
▲5642 Sea
Caucasus

Black Sea

Gobi
Desert

Huang He

Honshu

editerranean Sea

Suez
Canal

The Gulf

Arabian
Peninsula

Kunlun Shan

H i m a l a y a

8848 ▲ Mount
Everest

R. Indus

R. Ganges

Chang Jiang

East
China
Sea

Tropic of Cancer

hara

R. Nile

Red Sea

Arabian
Sea

Bay
of
Bengal

South
China
Sea

PACIFIC

FRICA

R. Congo

Lake
Victoria

Kilimanjaro
▲ 5892

I N D I A N

Sumatra

Borneo

Java

Puncak Jaya
▲
5030

New Guinea

OCEAN

Equator

Madagascar

O C E A N

Kalahari
Desert

Drakensberg

O C E A N I A

Australia

Lake
Eyre

R. Darling

Tropic of Capricorn

Cape of
Good Hope

R. Murray

Tasman
Sea

New
Zealand

SOUTHERN OCEAN

Antarctic Circle

ANTARCTICA

South America

Antarctica

Europe

Oceania

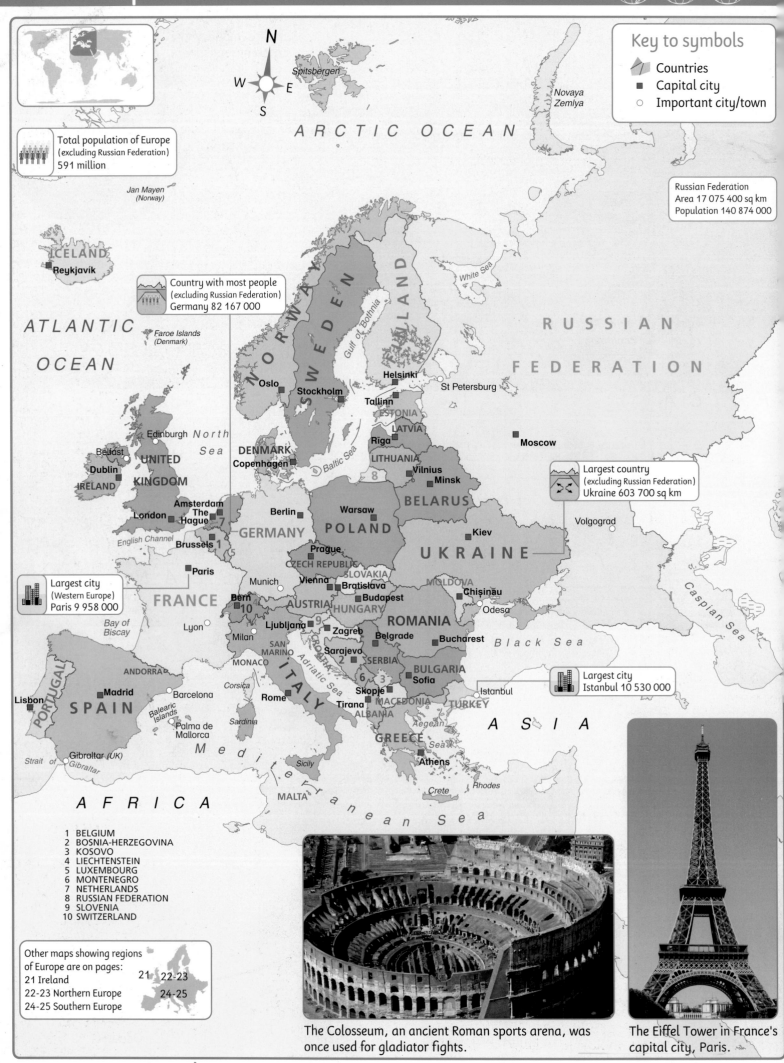

Key to symbols
- Countries
- ■ Capital city
- ○ Important city/town

Total population of Europe
(excluding Russian Federation)
591 million

Russian Federation
Area 17 075 400 sq km
Population 140 874 000

ARCTIC OCEAN

Spitsbergen

Jan Mayen
(Norway)

Novaya
Zemlya

Country with most people
(excluding Russian Federation)
Germany 82 167 000

ATLANTIC

OCEAN

Faroe Islands
(Denmark)

ICELAND
■ Reykjavík

White Sea

RUSSIAN

FEDERATION

NORWAY
SWEDEN
FINLAND

Oslo ■
Stockholm ■

Helsinki ■
○ St Petersburg

Tallinn ■
ESTONIA

■ Moscow

Edinburgh ○ North
Sea

Belfast ○
UNITED
Dublin ■
KINGDOM
IRELAND

DENMARK
Copenhagen ■

Baltic Sea

Riga ■
LATVIA

LITHUANIA
Vilnius ■
8

Largest country
(excluding Russian Federation)
Ukraine 603 700 sq km

Amsterdam ■
London ■ The 7
Hague
English Channel

Berlin ■
GERMANY

Warsaw ■
POLAND

Minsk ■
BELARUS

Volgograd ○

Brussels ■ 1
5

Prague ■
CZECH REPUBLIC

Kiev ■
UKRAINE

Caspian Sea

■ Paris

Munich ○
Vienna ○
Bratislava ■
SLOVAKIA

Largest city
(Western Europe)
Paris 9 958 000

FRANCE

Bern ■
10

AUSTRIA
Budapest ■
HUNGARY

MOLDOVA
Chișinău ■

Lyon ○

Ljubljana ■ 9
Zagreb ■
○ Odesa

Milan ○
SAN
MARINO
Sarajevo ■
2
Belgrade ■
SERBIA
Bucharest ■
ROMANIA

Black Sea

Bay of
Biscay

Corsica
Rome ■
ITALY
Adriatic Sea
6 3
Skopje ■
Sofia ■
BULGARIA

MONACO

ANDORRA

Madrid ■
SPAIN

Barcelona ○

Balearic
Islands
Palma de
Mallorca

Sardinia

Tirana ■
MACEDONIA
ALBANIA
Istanbul ○
TURKEY

ASIA

Largest city
Istanbul 10 530 000

PORTUGAL
Lisbon ■

Gibraltar (UK)
Strait of
Gibraltar

Sicily

Mediterranean Sea

GREECE
Aegean
Sea

Athens ■

Crete
Rhodes

AFRICA

MALTA

1 BELGIUM
2 BOSNIA-HERZEGOVINA
3 KOSOVO
4 LIECHTENSTEIN
5 LUXEMBOURG
6 MONTENEGRO
7 NETHERLANDS
8 RUSSIAN FEDERATION
9 SLOVENIA
10 SWITZERLAND

Other maps showing regions
of Europe are on pages:
21 Ireland
22-23 Northern Europe
24-25 Southern Europe

21 22-23
24-25

The Colosseum, an ancient Roman sports arena, was
once used for gladiator fights.

The Eiffel Tower in France's
capital city, Paris.

0   250   500   750   1000   1250 km

Scale : One centimetre on this map is the same as 250 kilometres on the ground.

Total area of Europe
9 908 599 sq km

Largest island
Great Britain 218 476 sq km

Longest river
Volga 3688 km

Highest mountain
El'brus 5642 m

Largest lake
Caspian Sea 371 000 sq km

Key to symbols

Land height above sea level in metres

over 5000
2000 – 5000
1000 – 2000
500 – 1000
200 – 500
0 – 200

El'brus
5642 ▲ Mountain and height in metres

〜 River

Lake

Seasonal lake

Ice cap

Land below sea level

Mount Etna, on the island of Sicily, is one of the world's most active volcanoes.

Narrow, steep sided inlets called fjords are found along much of the Norwegian coastline.

0   250   500   750   1000   1250 km

Scale : One centimetre on this map is the same as 250 kilometres on the ground.

European Union

The European Union (EU) was created in 1957 by the Treaty of Rome. The original members of the then European Economic Community (EEC) were Belgium, France, West Germany, Italy, Luxembourg and the Netherlands. Since 1957 the EU has grown and now has 27 member states. The total population of the EU is now nearly half a billion.

The headquarters of the EU in the Belgian capital, Brussels.

EU member
EU applicant
Non EU member

B.-H.	BOSNIA-HERZEGOVINA
KOS.	KOSOVO
L.	LIECHTENSTEIN
LUX.	LUXEMBOURG
MAC.	MACEDONIA
MOL.	MOLDOVA
MON.	MONTENEGRO
R.F.	RUSSIAN FEDERATION
SL.	SLOVENIA
SWITZ.	SWITZERLAND

ICELAND
NORWAY
SWEDEN
FINLAND
ESTONIA
LATVIA
LITHUANIA
R.F.
UNITED KINGDOM
IRELAND
DENMARK
BELARUS
NETHERLANDS
GERMANY
POLAND
BELGIUM
LUX.
CZECH REPUBLIC
UKRAINE
SLOVAKIA
L.
AUSTRIA
HUNGARY
MOL.
SWITZ.
FRANCE
SL.
CROATIA
ROMANIA
B.-H.
SERBIA
PORTUGAL
ANDORRA
MON.
KOS.
BULGARIA
ITALY
MAC.
ALBANIA
SPAIN
TURKEY
GREECE
MALTA
CYPRUS

Austria
Belgium
Bulgaria
Cyprus
Czech Republic
Denmark
Estonia
Finland
France
Germany
Greece
Hungary
Ireland
Italy
Latvia
Lithuania
Luxembourg
Malta
Netherlands
Poland
Portugal
Romania
Slovakia
Slovenia
Spain
Sweden
United Kingdom

Key to symbols

◤ Countries
■ Capital city
○ Important city/town

Other maps showing regions of the
United Kingdom are on pages:
18-19 England and Wales
20 Scotland
21 Northern Ireland

20
21
18-19

N
W · E
S

Shetland
Islands

ATLANTIC
OCEAN

Orkney
Islands

Outer Hebrides

Inverness

Aberdeen

Fort William

SCOTLAND

Dundee

North

Glasgow   ■ Edinburgh

Sea

Londonderry

NORTHERN
IRELAND   ■ Belfast

Newcastle
upon Tyne

UNITED

Middlesbrough

Dundalk

Isle of
Man

Irish Sea

York

Blackpool   Bradford   Leeds
Preston

IRELAND

Manchester

Liverpool   Sheffield

Galway   ■ Dublin

KINGDOM

Stoke-on-Trent   Derby   Nottingham

Limerick

ENGLAND   Norwich

Wolverhampton   Leicester

WALES   Birmingham

Waterford

Coventry   Cambridge

Ipswich

Cork

Oxford

■ London   Southend-on-Sea

Swansea

Celtic Sea

Bristol   Reading

■ Cardiff

BELGIUM

Southampton   Brighton
Portsmouth
Bournemouth

Plymouth   Torquay

English Channel

Channel
Islands

FRANCE

Tower Bridge crosses the River Thames in London.

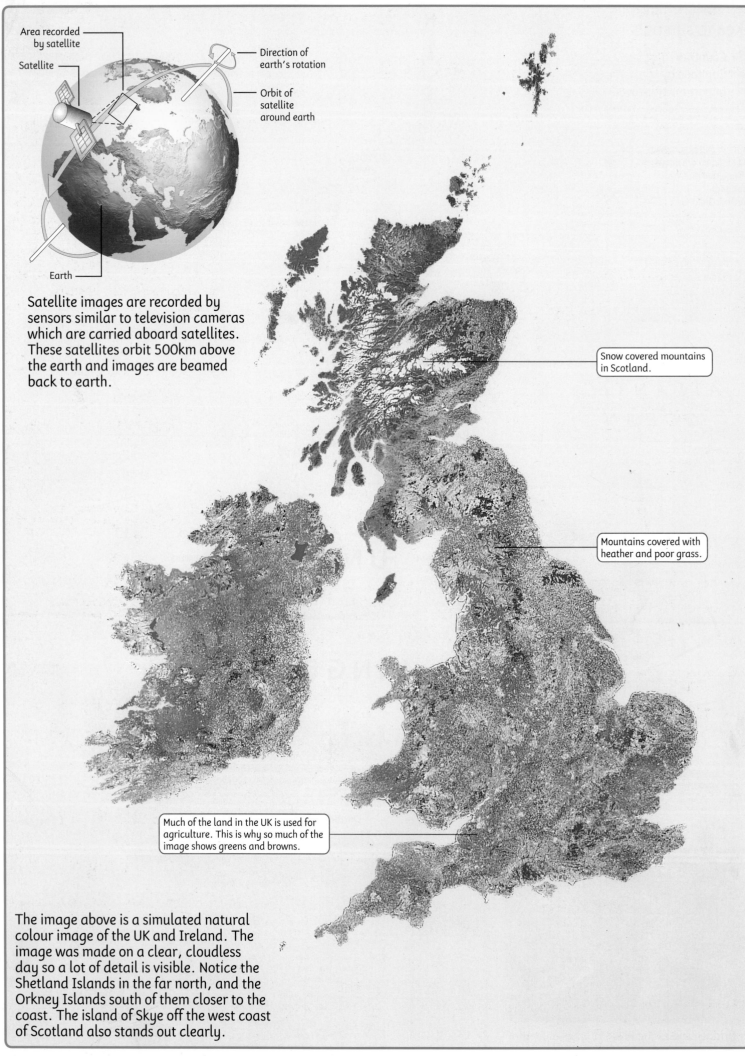

Area recorded by satellite

Satellite

Direction of earth's rotation

Orbit of satellite around earth

Earth

Satellite images are recorded by sensors similar to television cameras which are carried aboard satellites. These satellites orbit 500km above the earth and images are beamed back to earth.

Snow covered mountains in Scotland.

Mountains covered with heather and poor grass.

Much of the land in the UK is used for agriculture. This is why so much of the image shows greens and browns.

The image above is a simulated natural colour image of the UK and Ireland. The image was made on a clear, cloudless day so a lot of detail is visible. Notice the Shetland Islands in the far north, and the Orkney Islands south of them closer to the coast. The island of Skye off the west coast of Scotland also stands out clearly.

Key to symbols

Land height above sea level in metres

- over 1000
- 500 – 1000
- 200 – 500
- 100 – 200
- 0 – 100

Ben Nevis
▲
1344 Mountain and height in metres

〰 River

☁ Lake

▨ Land below sea level

⬚ Total area of the United Kingdom 244 082 sq km

N
W ✦ E
S

Shetland Islands
Mainland
Sumburgh Head

One of Scotland's famous glens, Glencoe.

Orkney Islands
Mainland
Hoy
Pentland Firth
Cape Wrath
Duncansby Head

Outer Hebrides
Isle of Lewis
Harris
St Kilda
North Uist
Skye
South Uist
Rum
Coll
Tiree
Inner Hebrides
The Minch
North West Highlands

Moray Firth
R. Spey
Loch Ness
Cairngorm Mts
R. Dee
Ben Macdui 1309 ▲
Ben Nevis 1344 ▲
Grampian Mts
Ben More 966 ▲
Glen Coe
Mull
Loch Tay
R. Tay
Loch Lomond
Ochil Hills
Jura
R. Forth
Firth of Forth
Islay
R. Clyde
Arran
Firth of Clyde

⛰ Highest mountain Ben Nevis 1344 m

ATLANTIC OCEAN

☁ Largest lake Lough Neagh 396 sq km

Malin Head
R. Foyle
Lower Lough Erne
Lough Neagh
Antrim Hills
R. Bann
North Channel
Donegal Bay
Upper Lough Erne
Mourne Mts
Slieve Donard 852 ▲
Dundalk Bay
Achill I.
Lough Mask
Lough Corrib
Ireland
Lough Ree
R. Shannon
R. Boyne
Galway Bay
Lough Derg
Lugnaquilla Mtn 926 ▲
Wicklow Mts
R. Barrow
R. Shannon
R. Suir
Carrantuohill 1041 ▲
R. Blackwater
Cape Clear

Southern Uplands
Merrick 843 ▲
R. Tweed
Cheviot Hills
Solway Firth
R. Tyne
Scafell Pike 977 ▲
Lake District
Great
R. Tees
North York Moors
Flamborough Head
R. Ouse
Spurn Head
R. Mersey
High Peak
Kinder Scout 636 ▲
R. Trent
Britain
Pennines

⬡ Largest island Great Britain 218 476 sq km

North Sea

Isle of Man
Irish Sea

Anglesey
Snowdon 1085 ▲
R. Dee
Cambrian Mountains
Cardigan Bay
Black Mountains 886 ▲
Brecon Beacons
R. Wye
R. Severn
R. Severn
Cotswold Hills
R. Avon
The Fens
Norfolk Broads
R. Great Ouse
Chiltern Hills
R. Thames
R. Thames
North Downs
South Downs
Beachy Head
The Wash

〰 Longest river River Severn 354 km

St George's Channel
St David's Head
Celtic Sea
Bristol Channel
Exmoor
Mendip Hills
Bodmin Moor
Dartmoor
Yes Tor 619 ▲
R. Tamar
Lyme Bay
Isle of Wight
Start Point
Land's End
Isles of Scilly

English Channel

Channel Islands

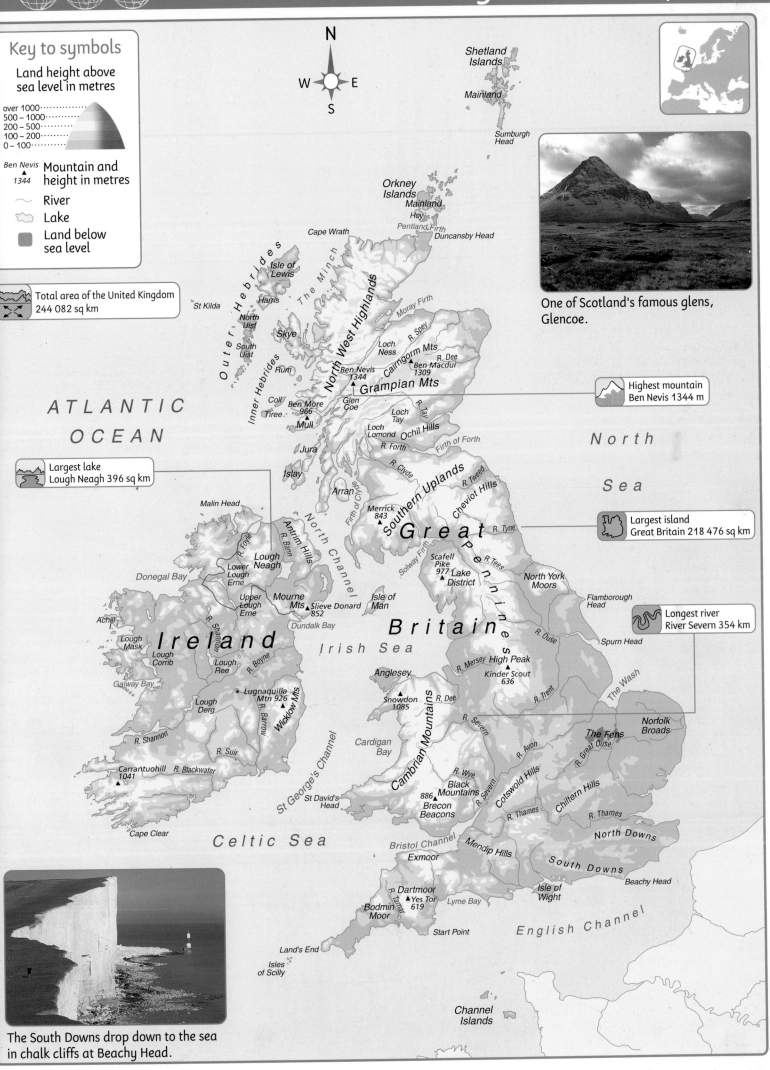

The South Downs drop down to the sea in chalk cliffs at Beachy Head.

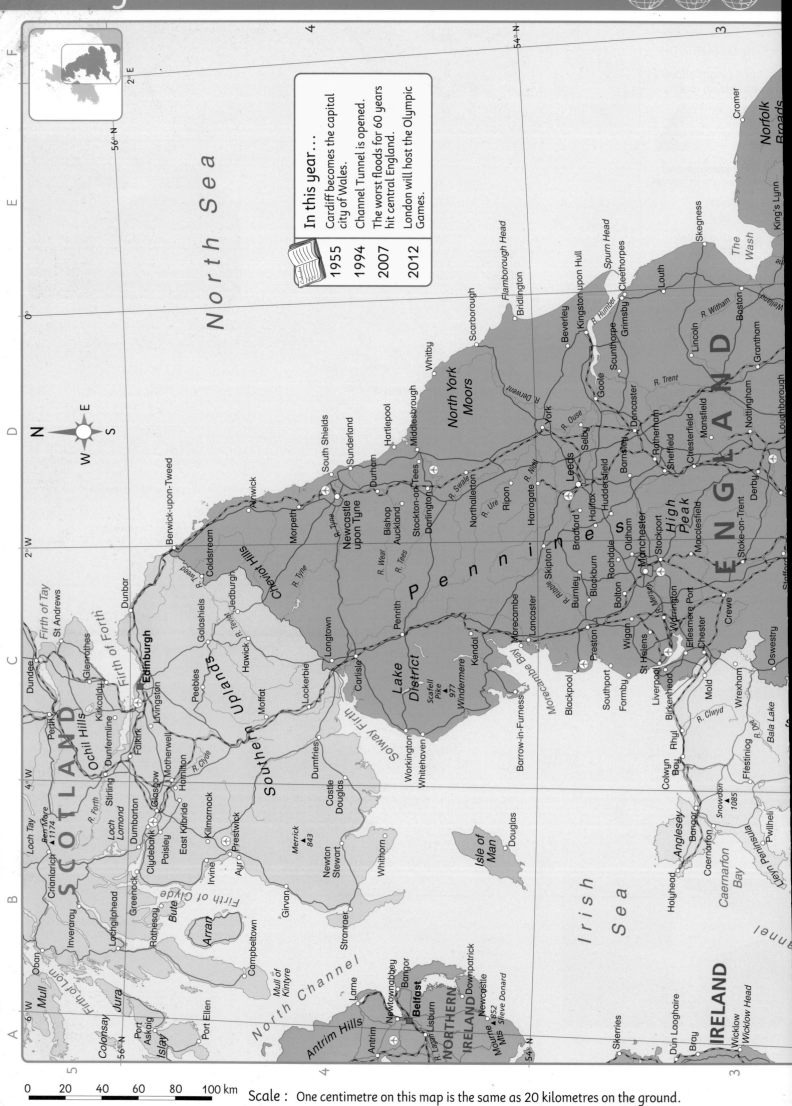

In this year...

1955	Cardiff becomes the capital city of Wales.
1994	Channel Tunnel is opened.
2007	The worst floods for 60 years hit central England.
2012	London will host the Olympic Games.

Scale : One centimetre on this map is the same as 20 kilometres on the ground.

0 20 40 60 80 100 km

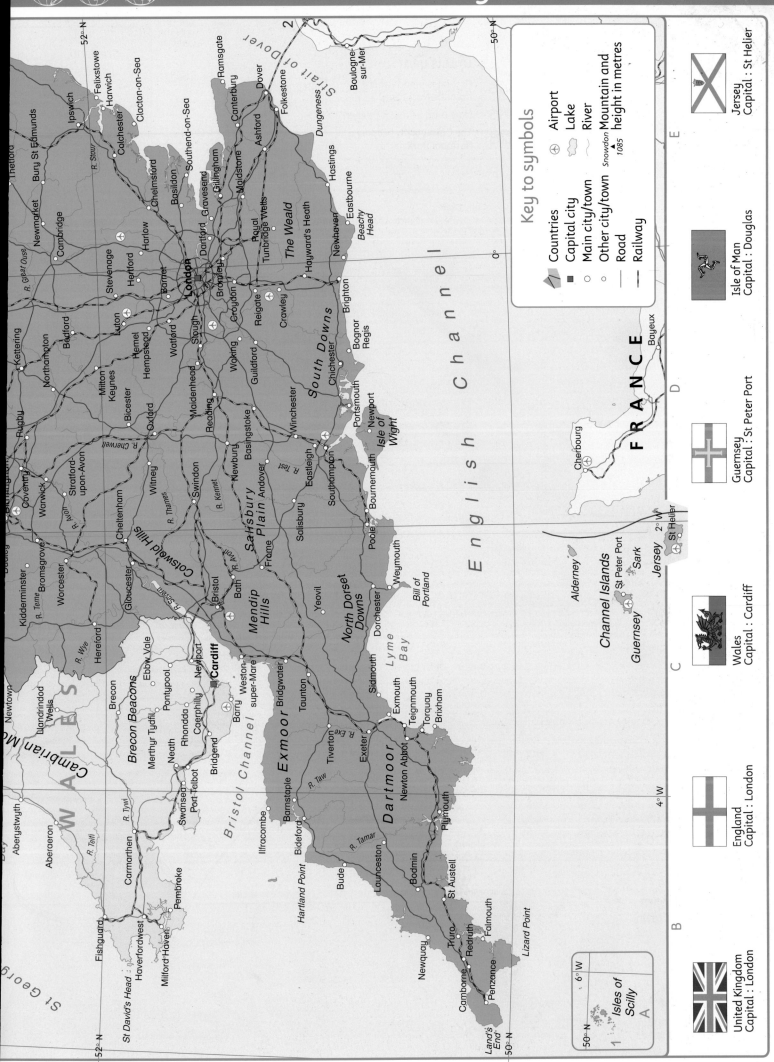

Key to symbols

Countries	⊕ Airport
■ Capital city	Lake
○ Main city/town	~ River
○ Other city/town	▲ *Snowdon* Mountain and
— Road	1085 height in metres
Railway	

United Kingdom
Capital : London

England
Capital : London

Wales
Capital : Cardiff

Guernsey
Capital : St Peter Port

Isle of Man
Capital : Douglas

Jersey
Capital : St Helier

Scotland
Capital : Edinburgh

In this year...

1975	First oil is piped ashore from the North Sea.
1995	Skye road bridge is opened.
2003	The Cairngorms become a National Park.

Key to symbols

◹ Countries
■ Capital city
○ Main city/town
○ Other city/town
— Road
┄ Railway
✈ Airport
▱ Lake
— River
▲ Ben Nevis 1344 Mountain and height in metres

Scale : One centimetre on this map is the same as 20 kilometres on the ground.

0 20 40 60 80 100 km

Key to symbols

- Countries
- ■ Capital city
- ○ Main city/town
- ○ Other city/town
- — Road
- —+— Railway
- ⊕ Airport
- Lake
- River
- *Carrantuohill* ▲ Mountain and
  1041 height in metres

In this year...

1920	Ireland becomes an independent country.
2002	Ireland adopts the euro as its currency.
2005	Ireland's first offshore wind farm is switched on at Arklow Bank.

Ireland
Capital : Dublin

Northern Ireland
Capital : Belfast

In this year...

1963   A volcanic eruption causes the formation of a new island, Surtsey, near Iceland.

1999   Euro is introduced as the single currency.

2004   First Eastern European countries join the EU.

Key to symbols

- Countries
- Capital city
- Main city/town
- Other city/town
- Road
- Railway
- Canal
- Airport
- Lake
- River
- *Galdhøpiggen* 2470   Mountain and height in metres

Scale : One centimetre on this map is the same as 100 kilometres on the ground.

0   100   200   300   400   500 km

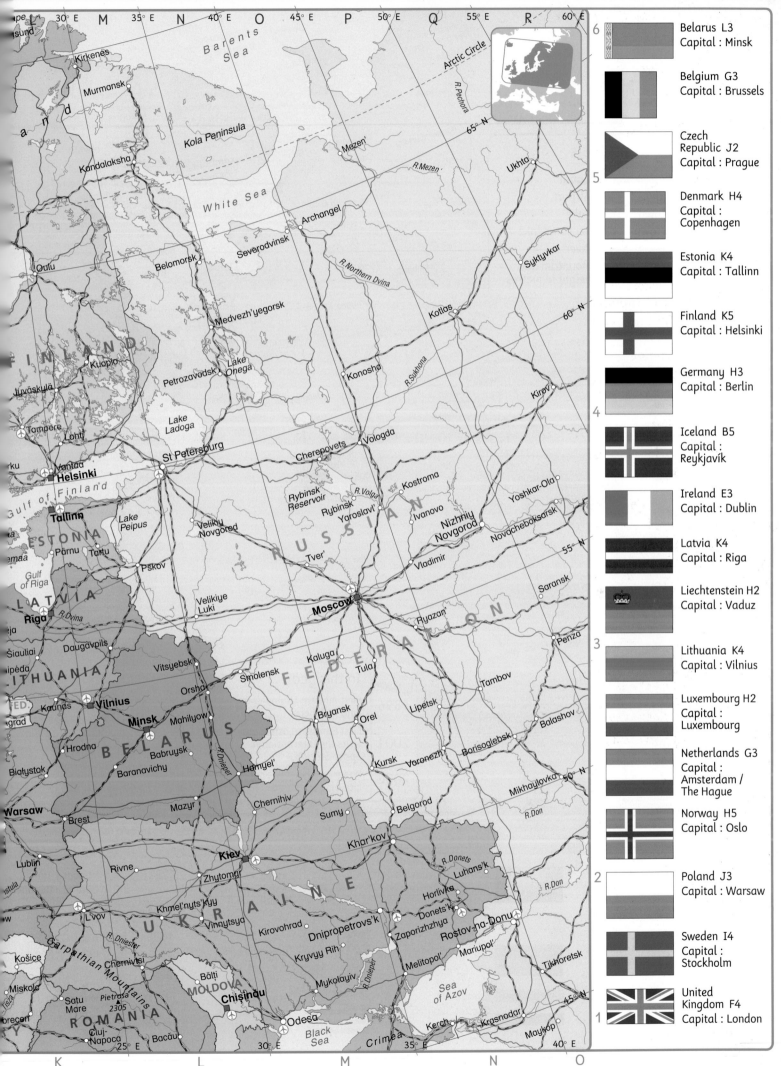

Belarus L3
Capital : Minsk

Belgium G3
Capital : Brussels

Czech Republic J2
Capital : Prague

Denmark H4
Capital : Copenhagen

Estonia K4
Capital : Tallinn

Finland K5
Capital : Helsinki

Germany H3
Capital : Berlin

Iceland B5
Capital : Reykjavík

Ireland E3
Capital : Dublin

Latvia K4
Capital : Riga

Liechtenstein H2
Capital : Vaduz

Lithuania K4
Capital : Vilnius

Luxembourg H2
Capital : Luxembourg

Netherlands G3
Capital : Amsterdam / The Hague

Norway H5
Capital : Oslo

Poland J3
Capital : Warsaw

Sweden I4
Capital : Stockholm

United Kingdom F4
Capital : London

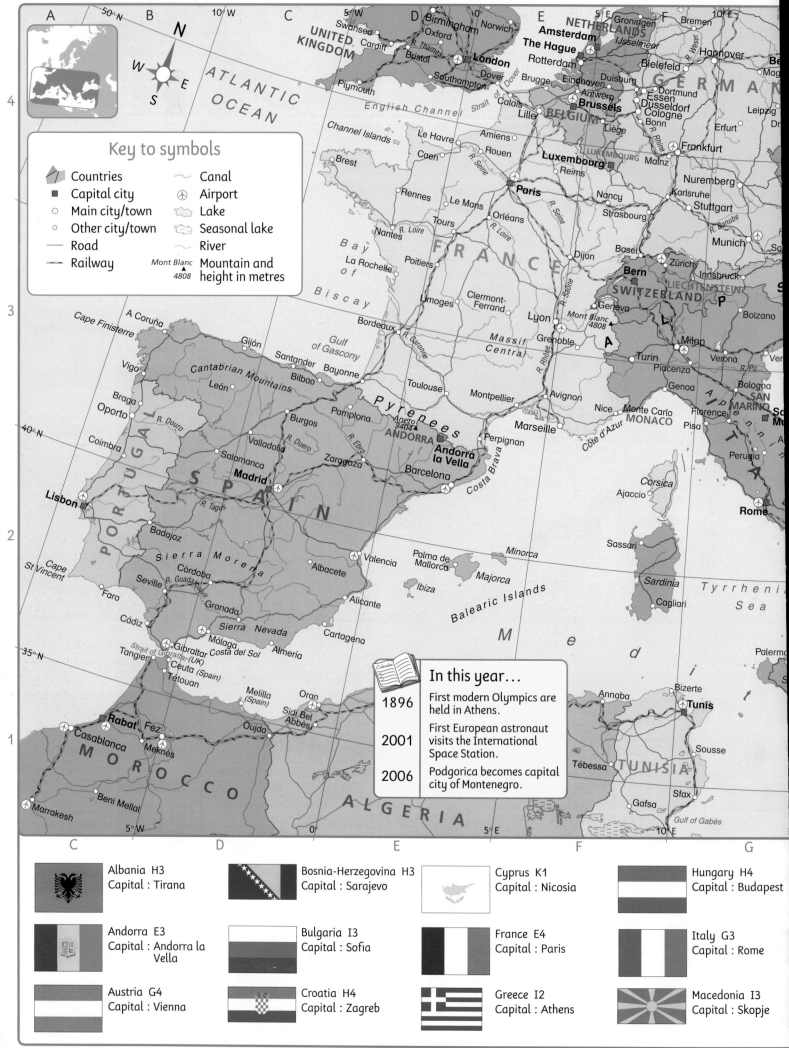

Key to symbols

Countries	Canal
Capital city	Airport
Main city/town	Lake
Other city/town	Seasonal lake
Road	River
Railway	Mont Blanc 4808 ▲ Mountain and height in metres

In this year...

1896	First modern Olympics are held in Athens.
2001	First European astronaut visits the International Space Station.
2006	Podgorica becomes capital city of Montenegro.

Albania H3
Capital : Tirana

Andorra E3
Capital : Andorra la Vella

Austria G4
Capital : Vienna

Bosnia-Herzegovina H3
Capital : Sarajevo

Bulgaria I3
Capital : Sofia

Croatia H4
Capital : Zagreb

Cyprus K1
Capital : Nicosia

France E4
Capital : Paris

Greece I2
Capital : Athens

Hungary H4
Capital : Budapest

Italy G3
Capital : Rome

Macedonia I3
Capital : Skopje

0   100   200   300   400   500 km

Scale : One centimetre on this map is the same as 100 kilometres on the ground.

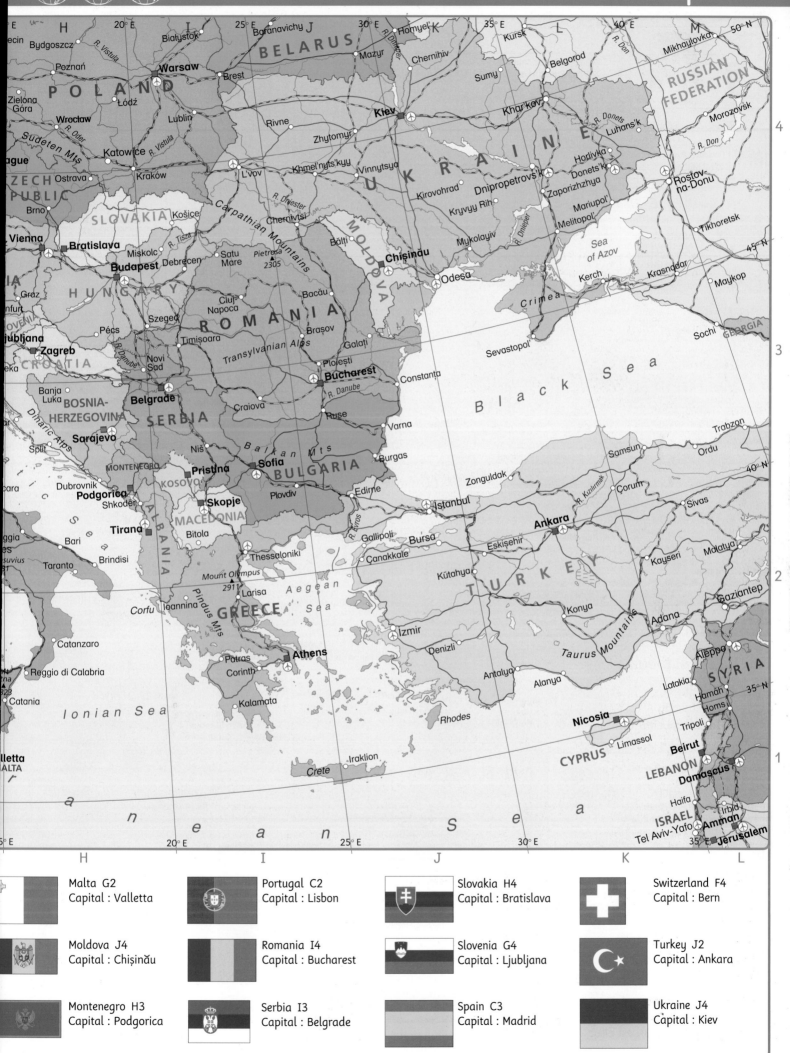

	Malta G2	Capital : Valletta
	Portugal C2	Capital : Lisbon
	Slovakia H4	Capital : Bratislava
	Switzerland F4	Capital : Bern
	Moldova J4	Capital : Chişinău
	Romania I4	Capital : Bucharest
	Slovenia G4	Capital : Ljubljana
	Turkey J2	Capital : Ankara
	Montenegro H3	Capital : Podgorica
	Serbia I3	Capital : Belgrade
	Spain C3	Capital : Madrid
	Ukraine J4	Capital : Kiev

Largest country
Russian Federation 17 075 400 sq km

Country with most people
China 1 330 265 000

Russian Federation
Area 17 075 400 sq km
Population 140 874 000

Total population of Asia
(including Russian Federation)
4262 million

Largest city
Tokyo 36 094 000

ARCTIC OCEAN

N
W E
S

EUROPE

St Petersburg

1 ARMENIA
2 AZERBAIJAN
3 KYRGYZSTAN
4 TAJIKISTAN

RUSSIAN FEDERATION

Moscow

Perm

Yakutsk

Sea of Okhotsk

Sakhalin

Chelyabinsk

Omsk

Novosibirsk

Irkutsk

Lake Baikal

Sapporo

Black Sea

Volgograd

KAZAKHSTAN

Astana

Ulan Bator

MONGOLIA

Harbin

Sea of Japan (East Sea)

JAPAN

Ankara

GEORGIA

T'bilisi

Aral Sea

Lake Balkhash

Shenyang

NORTH KOREA

Tokyo

TURKEY

Yerevan

Baku

UZBEKISTAN

Almaty

Ürümqi

Beijing

Pyongyang

Kobe

CYPRUS

LEBANON

SYRIA

Damascus

Tashkent

Bishkek

Tianjin

SOUTH KOREA

Seoul

Osaka

ISRAEL

Amman

TURKMENISTAN

Ashgabat

Fukuoka

JORDAN

Baghdad

Tehran

Dushanbe

Lanzhou

Xi'an

Nanjing

Shanghai

IRAQ

IRAN

Kabul

CHINA

Wuhan

KUWAIT

Kuwait

AFGHANISTAN

Islamabad

Lahore

Chongqing

Riyadh

BAHRAIN

QATAR

UNITED ARAB EMIRATES

PAKISTAN

Delhi

NEPAL

Kathmandu

Thimbu

BHUTAN

Guangzhou

Hong Kong

T'aipei

TAIWAN

PACIFIC OCEAN

SAUDI ARABIA

Muscat

New Delhi

Karachi

BANGLADESH

Luzon

San'a

YEMEN

OMAN

INDIA

Dhaka

Mandalay

Hanoi

PHILIPPINES

Aden

Mumbai

Hyderabad

Kolkata

MYANMAR (BURMA)

Nay Pyi Taw

Vientiane

LAOS

VIETNAM

South China Sea

Manila

AFRICA

Socotra (Yemen)

Arabian Sea

Chennai

Bay of Bengal

Yangon

THAILAND

Mindanao

Davao

Red Sea

Andaman Is (India)

Bangkok

CAMBODIA

Phnom Penh

Ho Chi Minh City

BRUNEI

Key to symbols

◣ Countries
■ Capital city
○ Important city/town

SRI LANKA

Sri Jayewardenepura Kotte

Colombo

Nicobar Is (India)

MALAYSIA

Kuala Lumpur

Putrajaya

Singapore

SINGAPORE

Borneo

Celebes

MALDIVES

Other maps showing regions of
Asia are on pages:
28-29 Russian Federation
30-31 Southwest and South Asia
32-33 East and Southeast Asia

28-29

30-31

32-33

INDONESIA

Makassar

Dili

EAST TIMOR

INDIAN OCEAN

Sumatra

Jakarta

Surabaya

Java

**The British Isles
at the same scale.**

AUSTRALIA

Shanghai is China's largest city.

A fruit stall in the Chinatown market place,
Kuala Lumpur, Malaysia.

0   500   1000   1500   2000   2500 km

Scale : One centimetre on this map is the same as 500 kilometres on the ground.

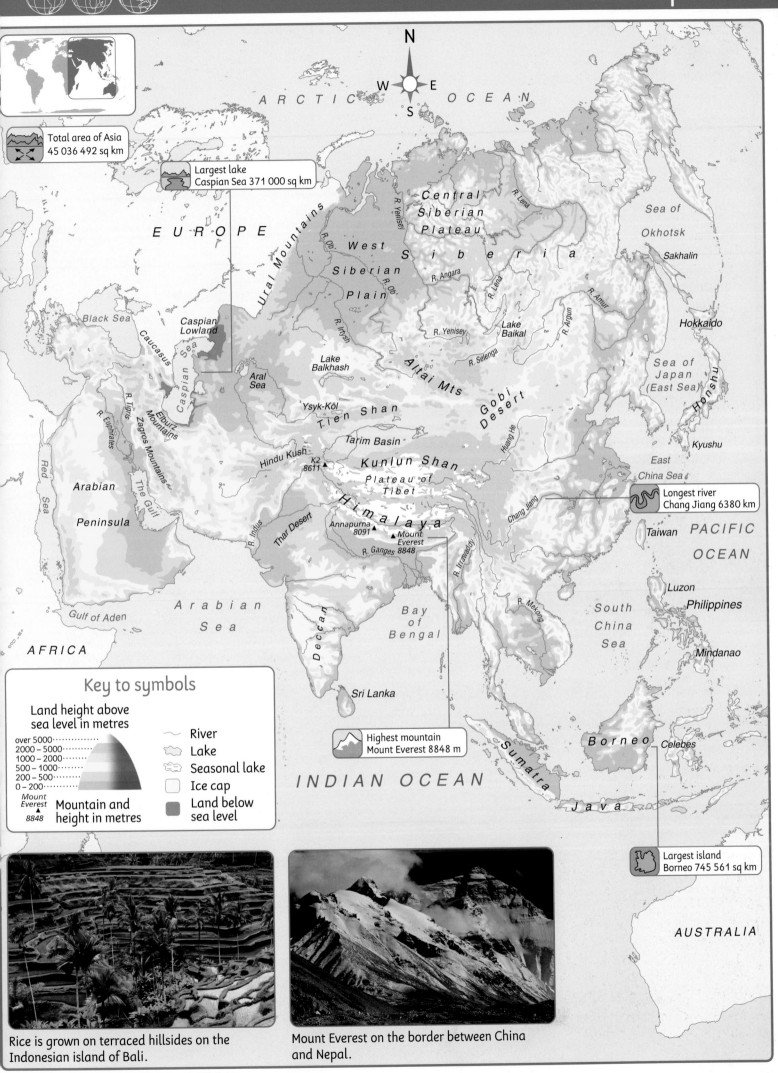

Total area of Asia
45 036 492 sq km

Largest lake
Caspian Sea 371 000 sq km

N
W E
S

A R C T I C O C E A N

E U R O P E

Ural Mountains

R. Yenisey

Central
Siberian
Plateau

R. Lena

S i b e r i a

Sea of
Okhotsk

West

R. Ob

Sakhalin

Black Sea

Caspian
Lowland

Siberian

Plain

R. Ob

R. Angara

R. Lena

R. Amur

Hokkaido

Caucasus

Caspian Sea

Aral
Sea

R. Irtysh

Lake
Balkhash

R. Yenisey

R. Selenga

Lake
Baikal

R. Argun

Altai Mts

Sea of
Japan
(East Sea)

R. Tigris

Elburz
Mountains

Ysyk-Köl

Gobi
Desert

Honshu

R. Euphrates

Zagros Mountains

T i e n S h a n

Huang He

Kyushu

Red
Sea

Arabian

The Gulf

Hindu Kush

Tarim Basin

Kunlun Shan

Plateau of
Tibet

East
China Sea

Longest river
Chang Jiang 6380 km

PACIFIC

OCEAN

Peninsula

R. Indus

Thar Desert

K2
8611 ▲

Himalaya

Annapurna
8091 ▲

▲ Mount
Everest
8848

R. Ganges

Chang Jiang

R. Irrawaddy

Taiwan

Gulf of Aden

A r a b i a n

S e a

Deccan

Bay
of
Bengal

R. Mekong

South
China
Sea

Luzon

Philippines

AFRICA

Mindanao

Sri Lanka

Highest mountain
Mount Everest 8848 m

Sumatra

B o r n e o

Celebes

INDIAN OCEAN

Java

Largest island
Borneo 745 561 sq km

Key to symbols

Land height above sea level in metres

over 5000
2000 – 5000
1000 – 2000
500 – 1000
200 – 500
0 – 200

Mount Everest
▲
8848
Mountain and
height in metres

～ River
Lake
Seasonal lake
Ice cap
Land below
sea level

AUSTRALIA

Rice is grown on terraced hillsides on the
Indonesian island of Bali.

Mount Everest on the border between China
and Nepal.

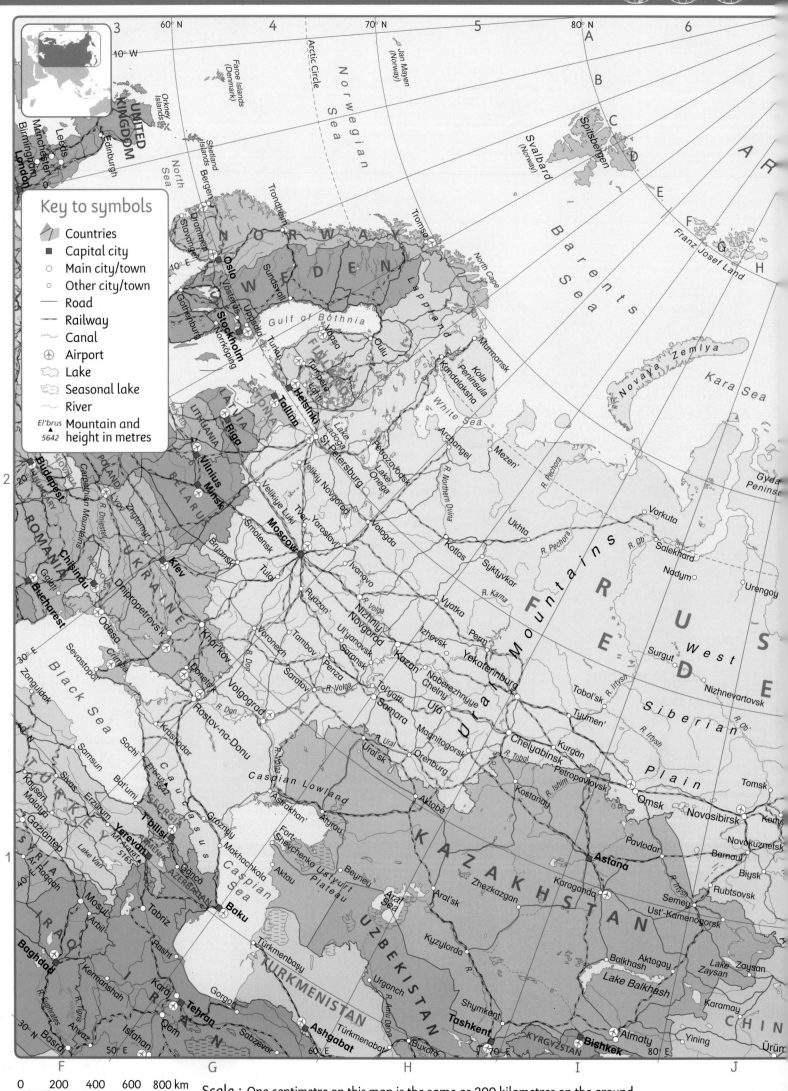

Key to symbols

- Countries
- ■ Capital city
- ○ Main city/town
- ○ Other city/town
- — Road
- Railway
- Canal
- ✈ Airport
- Lake
- Seasonal lake
- River
- El'brus ▲ 5642 Mountain and height in metres

Scale : One centimetre on this map is the same as 200 kilometres on the ground.

0   200   400   600   800 km

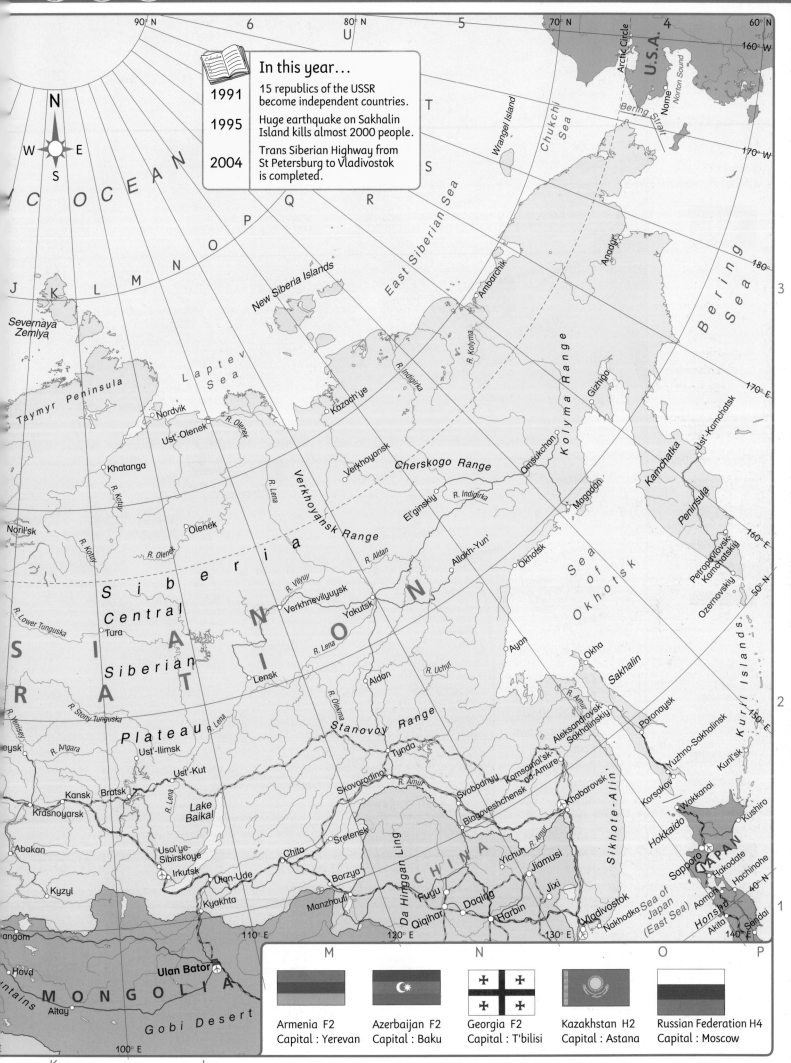

In this year...

1991 15 republics of the USSR become independent countries.

1995 Huge earthquake on Sakhalin Island kills almost 2000 people.

2004 Trans Siberian Highway from St Petersburg to Vladivostok is completed.

Armenia F2
Capital : Yerevan

Azerbaijan F2
Capital : Baku

Georgia F2
Capital : T'bilisi

Kazakhstan H2
Capital : Astana

Russian Federation H4
Capital : Moscow

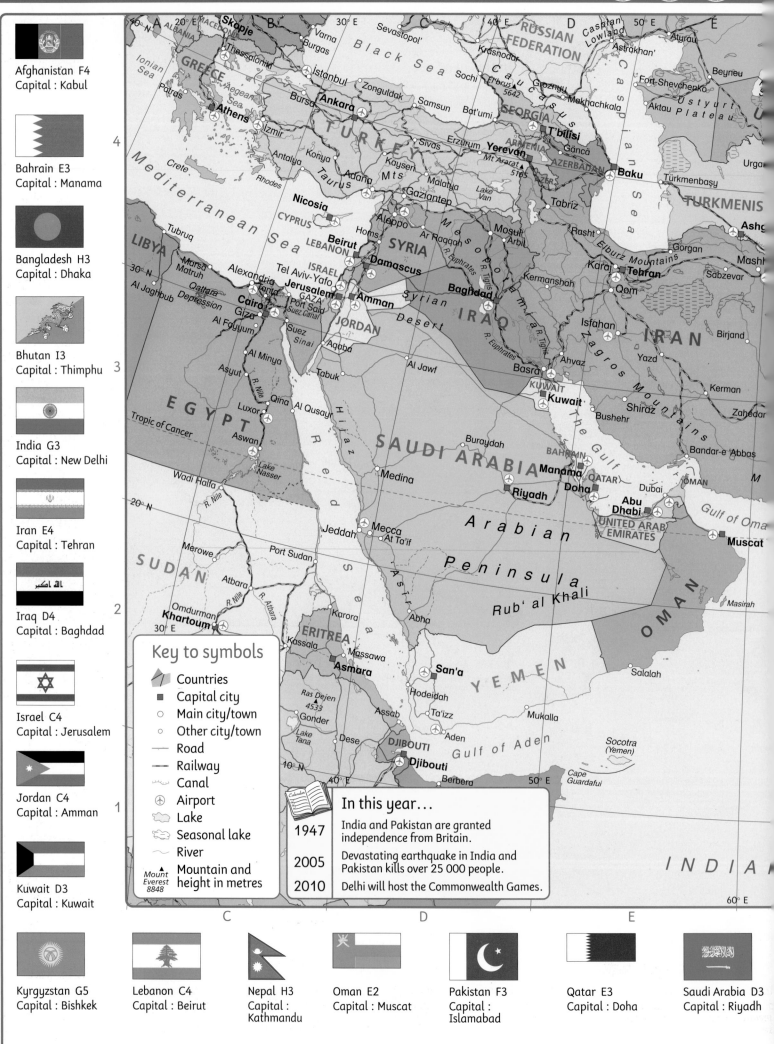

Afghanistan F4
Capital : Kabul

Bahrain E3
Capital : Manama

Bangladesh H3
Capital : Dhaka

Bhutan I3
Capital : Thimphu

India G3
Capital : New Delhi

Iran E4
Capital : Tehran

Iraq D4
Capital : Baghdad

Israel C4
Capital : Jerusalem

Jordan C4
Capital : Amman

Kuwait D3
Capital : Kuwait

Kyrgyzstan G5
Capital : Bishkek

Lebanon C4
Capital : Beirut

Nepal H3
Capital : Kathmandu

Oman E2
Capital : Muscat

Pakistan F3
Capital : Islamabad

Qatar E3
Capital : Doha

Saudi Arabia D3
Capital : Riyadh

Key to symbols

- Countries
- Capital city
- Main city/town
- Other city/town
- Road
- Railway
- Canal
- Airport
- Lake
- Seasonal lake
- River
- Mount Everest 8848 — Mountain and height in metres

In this year...

1947 — India and Pakistan are granted independence from Britain.

2005 — Devastating earthquake in India and Pakistan kills over 25 000 people.

2010 — Delhi will host the Commonwealth Games.

0 200 400 600 800 km

Scale : One centimetre on this map is the same as 200 kilometres on the ground.

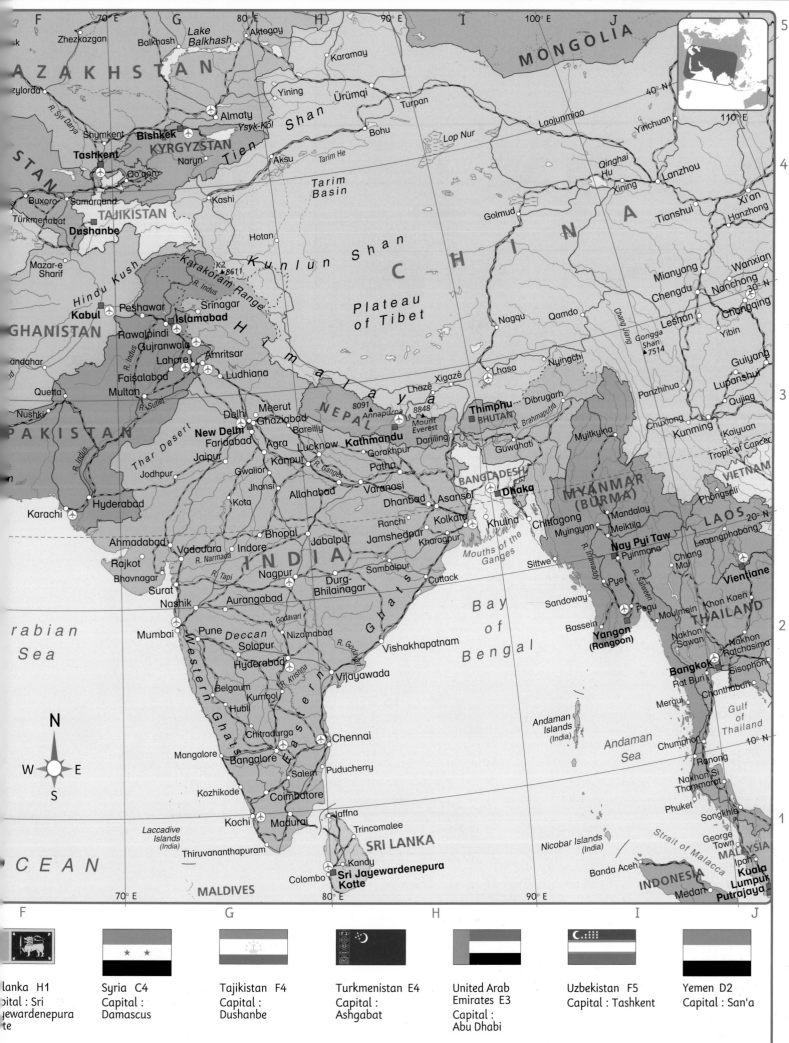

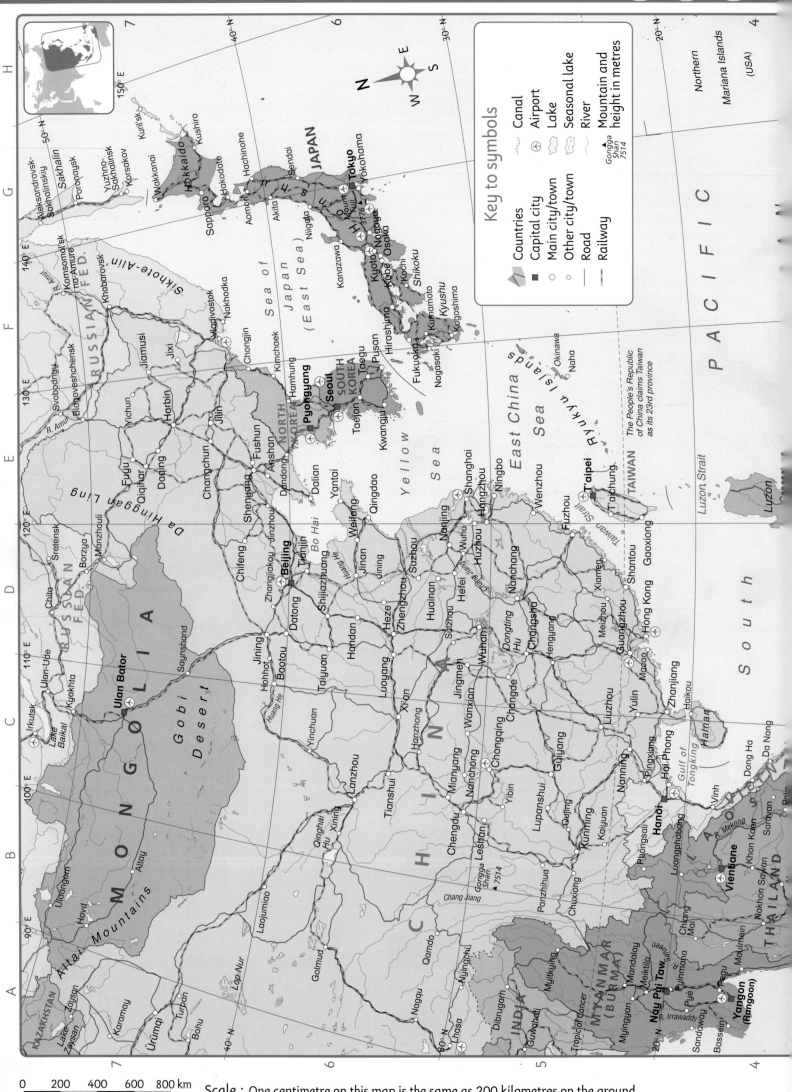

Key to symbols

Countries		Canal	
Capital city		Airport	
Main city/town		Lake	
Other city/town		Seasonal lake	
Road		River	
Railway		Mountain and height in metres	Gongga Shan 7514 ▲

Scale : One centimetre on this map is the same as 200 kilometres on the ground.

0   200   400   600   800 km

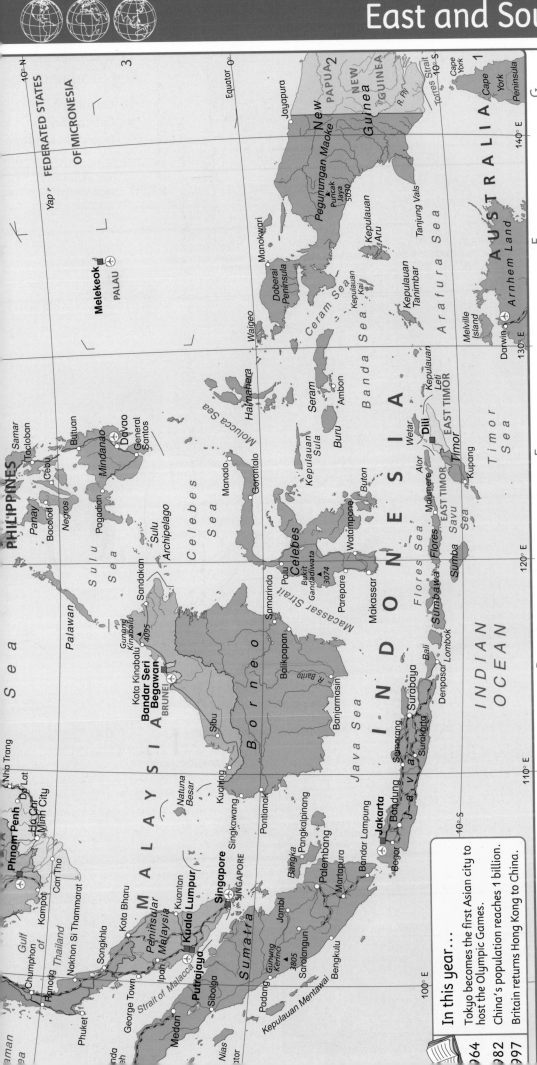

Mongolia B7
Capital : Ulan Bator

Vietnam C4
Capital : Hanoi

Malaysia C3
Capital : Putrajaya / Kuala Lumpur

Thailand B4
Capital : Bangkok

Laos C4
Capital : Vientiane

Taiwan E5
Capital : T'aipei

Japan G6
Capital : Tokyo

South Korea E6
Capital : Seoul

Indonesia D2
Capital : Jakarta

Singapore C3
Capital : Singapore

East Timor E2
Capital : Dili

Philippines E4
Capital : Manila

China B6
Capital : Beijing

Palau F3
Capital : Melekeok

Brunei D3
Capital : Bandar Seri Begawan

Cambodia C4
Capital : Phnom Penh

North Korea E7
Capital : Pyongyang

Myanmar B4
Capital : Yangon / Nay Pyi Taw

In this year...

Tokyo becomes the first Asian city to host the Olympic Games.

China's population reaches 1 billion.

Britain returns Hong Kong to China.

064

082

997

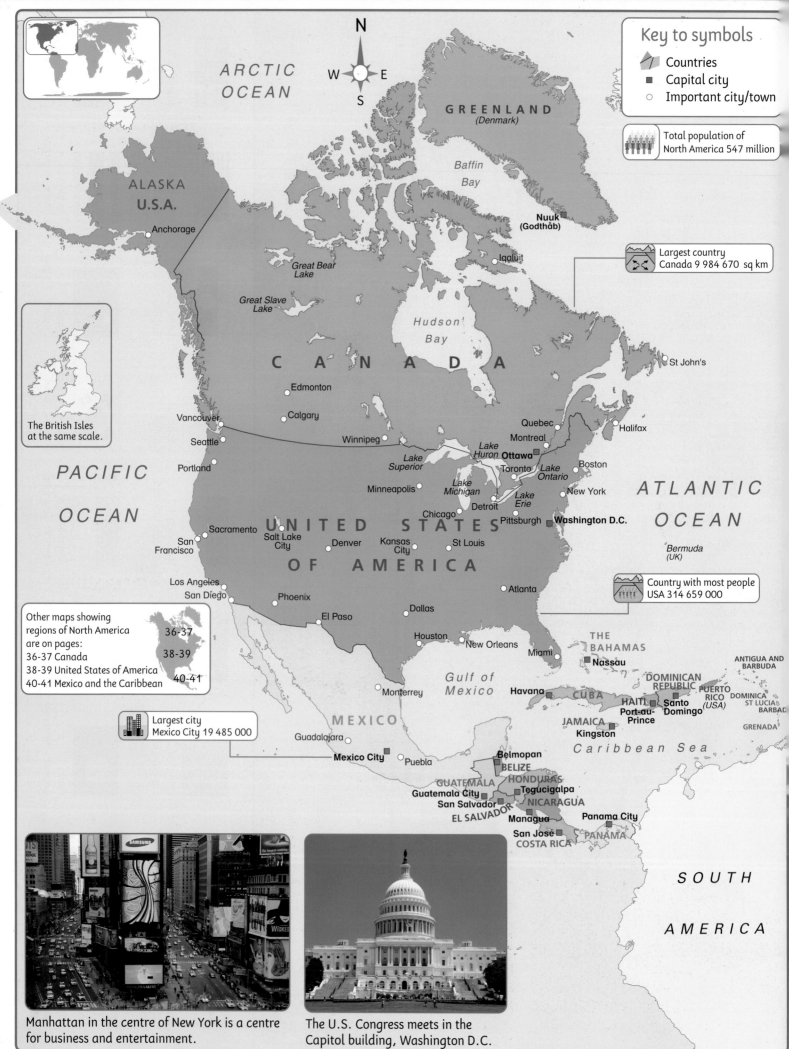

ARCTIC OCEAN

GREENLAND
(Denmark)

Baffin Bay

N
W E
S

Key to symbols
Countries
■ Capital city
○ Important city/town

Total population of
North America 547 million

ALASKA
U.S.A.

Anchorage

Nuuk
(Godthåb)

Iqaluit

Largest country
Canada 9 984 670 sq km

Great Bear Lake

Great Slave Lake

Hudson Bay

C A N A D A

St John's

The British Isles at the same scale.

Edmonton

Calgary

PACIFIC OCEAN

Vancouver

Seattle

Portland

Winnipeg

Quebec
Montreal

Halifax

Ottawa

Lake Huron
Lake Superior

Toronto

Lake Ontario

Boston

Lake Michigan

Lake Erie

New York

ATLANTIC OCEAN

Minneapolis

Detroit

Sacramento

Chicago

San Francisco

Salt Lake City

Denver

Kansas City

St Louis

Pittsburgh

Washington D.C.

U N I T E D   S T A T E S

O F   A M E R I C A

Bermuda
(UK)

Country with most people
USA 314 659 000

Los Angeles

San Diego

Phoenix

Atlanta

El Paso

Dallas

Other maps showing
regions of North America
are on pages:
36-37 Canada
38-39 United States of America
40-41 Mexico and the Caribbean

36-37
38-39
40-41

Houston

New Orleans

Miami

THE BAHAMAS

Nassau

Gulf of Mexico

ANTIGUA AND BARBUDA

Monterrey

M E X I C O

DOMINICAN REPUBLIC

Havana

CUBA

PUERTO RICO
(USA)

DOMINICA
ST LUCIA
BARBAD

Largest city
Mexico City 19 485 000

HAITI
Port-au-Prince

Santo Domingo

JAMAICA

GRENADA

Guadalajara

Kingston

Caribbean Sea

Mexico City

Puebla

Belmopan

BELIZE

HONDURAS

GUATEMALA

Guatemala City

Tegucigalpa

San Salvador

NICARAGUA

EL SALVADOR

Managua

Panama City

San José

PANAMA

COSTA RICA

SOUTH

AMERICA

Manhattan in the centre of New York is a centre
for business and entertainment.

The U.S. Congress meets in the
Capitol building, Washington D.C.

0   400   800   1200   1600   2000 km

Scale : One centimetre on this map is the same as 400 kilometres on the ground.

ASIA

ARCTIC OCEAN

N
W E
S

Iceland

Greenland

Ellesmere Island

Baffin Bay

Davis Strait

Cape Farewell

Total area of North America
24 680 331 sq km

Largest island
Greenland 2 175 600 sq km

Victoria Island

Baffin Island

R. Yukon

Mount McKinley 6194

R. Mackenzie

Great Bear Lake

Gulf of Alaska

Mount Logan 5959

Great Slave Lake

R. Peace

Hudson Bay

Labrador

Newfoundland

Largest lake
Lake Superior 82 100 sq km

Highest mountain
Mount McKinley 6194 m

Coast Mountains

3954 ▲

Rocky Mountains

Great Plains

Canadian Shield

PACIFIC OCEAN

R. St. Lawrence

Lake Superior

Lake Huron

Lake Ontario

Cape Cod

ATLANTIC OCEAN

Great Lakes

Niagara Falls

R. Snake

Lake Michigan

Lake Erie

Great Salt Lake

R. Missouri

R. North Platte

Mount Elbert 4398

R. Ohio

Appalachian Mountains

2037 ▲

Longest river
Mississippi-Missouri 5969 km

Great Basin

Mount Whitney 4418

R. Colorado

Grand Canyon

R. Red

R. Mississippi

Gulf of California

Sierra Madre Occidental

Sierra Madre Oriental

R. Brazos

Rio Grande

Florida

Gulf of Mexico

Cuba

Hispaniola

Yucatán

Caribbean Sea

Popocatépetl ▲ 5452

Lake Nicaragua

Isthmus of Panama

SOUTH AMERICA

Key to symbols

Land height above sea level in metres

over 5000
2000 – 5000
1000 – 2000
500 – 1000
200 – 500
0 – 200

Mount McKinley ▲ 6194 Mountain and height in metres

River

Lake

Seasonal lake

Polar ice cap

The Grand Canyon, a wide, deep gorge in the southwest of the USA.

The Niagara Falls, a set of massive waterfalls in Canada and the USA.

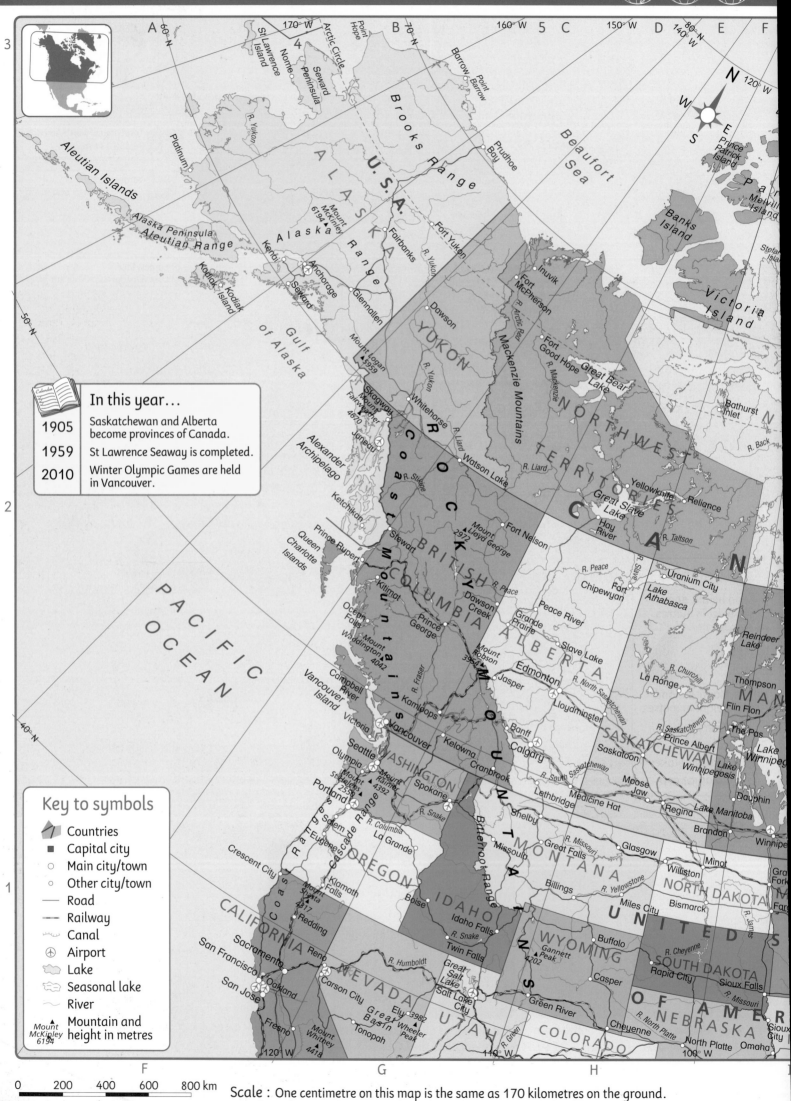

In this year…

1905	Saskatchewan and Alberta become provinces of Canada.
1959	St Lawrence Seaway is completed.
2010	Winter Olympic Games are held in Vancouver.

Key to symbols

- ◤ Countries
- ■ Capital city
- ○ Main city/town
- ○ Other city/town
- — Road
- —+— Railway
- ～ Canal
- ⊕ Airport
- ⬡ Lake
- ⬡ Seasonal lake
- ～ River
- ▲ Mountain and height in metres
  - Mount McKinley 6194

Scale : One centimetre on this map is the same as 170 kilometres on the ground.

0 200 400 600 800 km

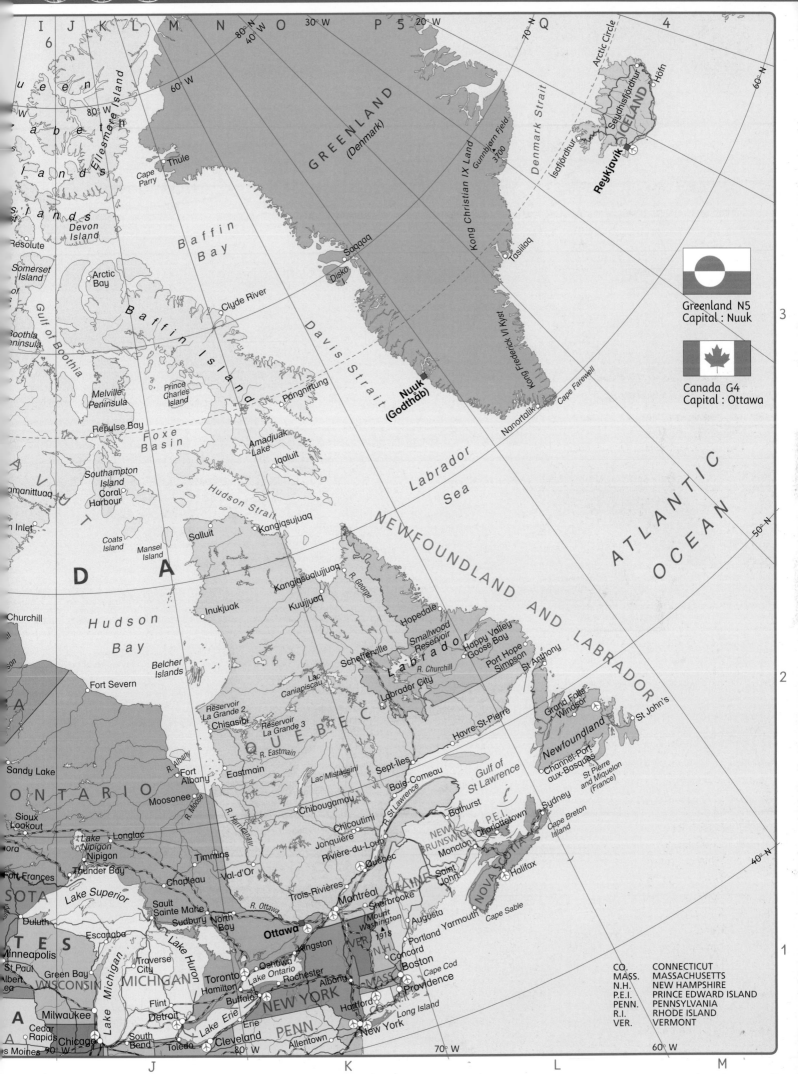

Greenland N5
Capital : Nuuk

Canada G4
Capital : Ottawa

CO.   CONNECTICUT
MASS.   MASSACHUSETTS
N.H.   NEW HAMPSHIRE
P.E.I.   PRINCE EDWARD ISLAND
PENN.   PENNSYLVANIA
R.I.   RHODE ISLAND
VER.   VERMONT

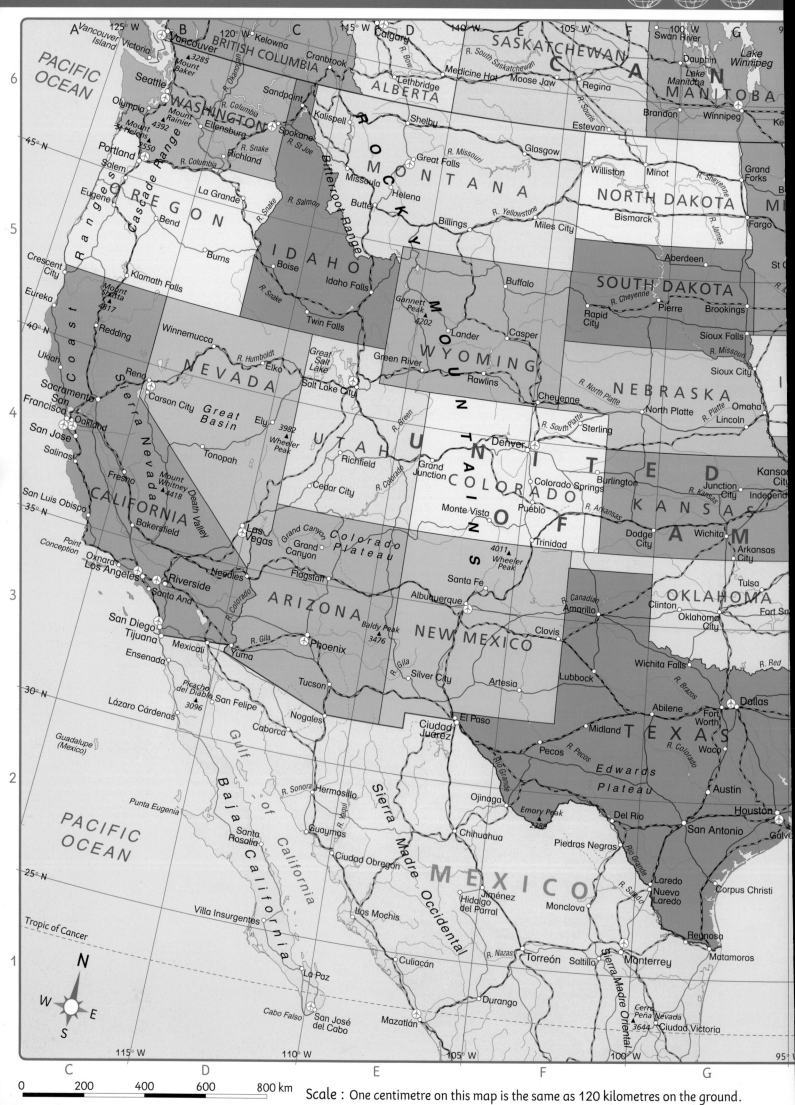

Scale : One centimetre on this map is the same as 120 kilometres on the ground.

0   200   400   600   800 km

Key to symbols

- ◤ Countries
- ▪ Capital city
- ○ Main city/town
- ○ Other city/town
- — Road
- ┼ Railway
- ⌇ Canal
- ✈ Airport
- ◠ Lake
- ◠ Seasonal lake
- ～ River
- ▲ Mountain and height in metres

Mount Whitney 4418

CO. CONNECTICUT
MASS. MASSACHUSETTS
N.H. NEW HAMPSHIRE
P.E.I. PRINCE EDWARD ISLAND
R.I. RHODE ISLAND
VER. VERMONT

United States of America D4
Capital : Washington D.C.

In this year...

1886	Statue of Liberty is erected on Liberty Island, New York.
2001	The September 11 attacks destroy the World Trade Center in New York City.
2005	Hurricane Katrina devastates New Orleans and parts of the Gulf Coast.
2009	Barack Obama becomes the USA's first black president.

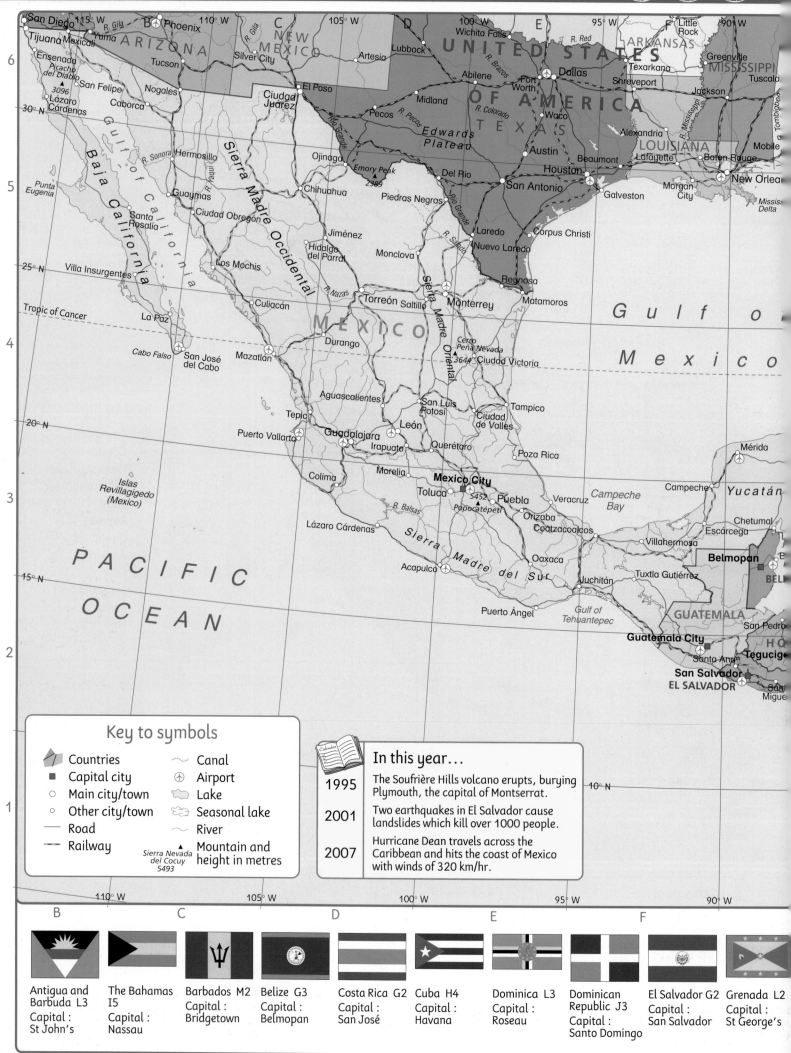

Key to symbols

Countries
Capital city
Main city/town
Other city/town
Road
Railway

Canal
Airport
Lake
Seasonal lake
River
Sierra Nevada del Cocuy 5493 ▲ Mountain and height in metres

In this year...

1995	The Soufrière Hills volcano erupts, burying Plymouth, the capital of Montserrat.
2001	Two earthquakes in El Salvador cause landslides which kill over 1000 people.
2007	Hurricane Dean travels across the Caribbean and hits the coast of Mexico with winds of 320 km/hr.

Antigua and Barbuda L3
Capital : St John's

The Bahamas I5
Capital : Nassau

Barbados M2
Capital : Bridgetown

Belize G3
Capital : Belmopan

Costa Rica G2
Capital : San José

Cuba H4
Capital : Havana

Dominica L3
Capital : Roseau

Dominican Republic J3
Capital : Santo Domingo

El Salvador G2
Capital : San Salvador

Grenada L2
Capital : St George's

0 200 400 600 800 km

Scale : One centimetre on this map is the same as 135 kilometres on the ground.

H I 75°W J 70°W K 65°W L M

Greenville 80°W Wilmington Cape Fear

Atlanta Columbia Charleston

Augusta SOUTH CAROLINA

Columbus Savannah Bermuda (UK) Hamilton 6

GEORGIA

Valdosta Jacksonville 30°N 60°W M

Lake City 5

FLORIDA Daytona Beach

ATLANTIC OCEAN

Orlando Cape Canaveral

St Petersburg Tampa

Lake Okeechobee 25°N

West Palm Beach Grand Bahama

Fort Lauderdale Freeport City Great Abaco

Miami THE BAHAMAS Tropic of Cancer 4

Florida Keys New Providence Nassau

Straits of Florida Andros Cat Island

Long Island

Havana Matanzas Great Exuma Turks and Caicos Islands (UK) 20°N

Pinar del Rio Santa Clara Acklins Island

Guane CUBA Great Inagua Grand Turk

Cabo Antonio Camagüey Holguín Hispaniola Leeward Islands

Isla de la Juventud Bayamo Santiago Virgin Is (UK) Anguilla (UK) St-Martin (Fr.) 3

Sa Maestra Guantánamo Cap-Haïtien San Juan Sint Maarten (Neth.) ANTIGUA AND BARBUDA

Santiago de Cuba Port-de-Paix Pico Duarte Santo Domingo Virgin Is (USA) Barbuda St John's

Cayman Islands (UK) HAITI 3175 Ponce ST KITTS AND NEVIS Antigua

Montego Bay Port-au-Prince DOMINICAN REPUBLIC PUERTO RICO (USA) Montserrat (UK) Guadeloupe (Fr.)

JAMAICA Kingston Jérémie Antilles DOMINICA Roseau Windward 15°N

Caribbean Martinique (Fr.)

Castries ST LUCIA BARBADOS

Kingstown Bridgetown

Sea ST VINCENT AND THE GRENADINES

Lesser Antilles GRENADA 2

St George's TRINIDAD & TOBAGO Tobago

NICARAGUA Punta Gallinas Aruba (Neth.) Curaçao (Neth.) Port of Spain

Rio Grande Ríohacha Coro Cumaná Güiria Trinidad

Managua Barranquilla Maracaibo Caracas Barcelona Maturín 10°N

Lake Managua Cartagena Valledupar Barquisimeto Valencia Maracay R. Tigre Orinoco Delta

COSTA RICA Lake Maracaibo Acarigua El Tigre Ciudad Guayana

San José Sincelejo Barinas Ciudad Bolívar R. Orinoco Embalse de Guri

Chirripó Colón Montería San Fernando de Apure El Callao 1

3819 Panama City Turbo Cúcuta San Cristóbal VENEZUELA

David Aguadulce COLOMBIA Bucaramanga Guiana Highlands

PANAMA Medellín Sierra Nevada del Cocuy Llanos R. Meta

5493

85°W H 80°W I 75°W J 70°W K 65°W L

Guatemala F3
Capital :
Guatemala City

Haiti J3
Capital :
Port-au-Prince

Honduras G2
Capital :
Tegucigalpa

Jamaica I3
Capital :
Kingston

Mexico D4
Capital :
Mexico City

Nicaragua G2
Capital :
Managua

Panama H1
Capital :
Panama City

St Kitts and
Nevis L3
Capital :
Basseterre

St Lucia L2
Capital :
Castries

St Vincent and
the Grenadines
L2
Capital :
Kingstown

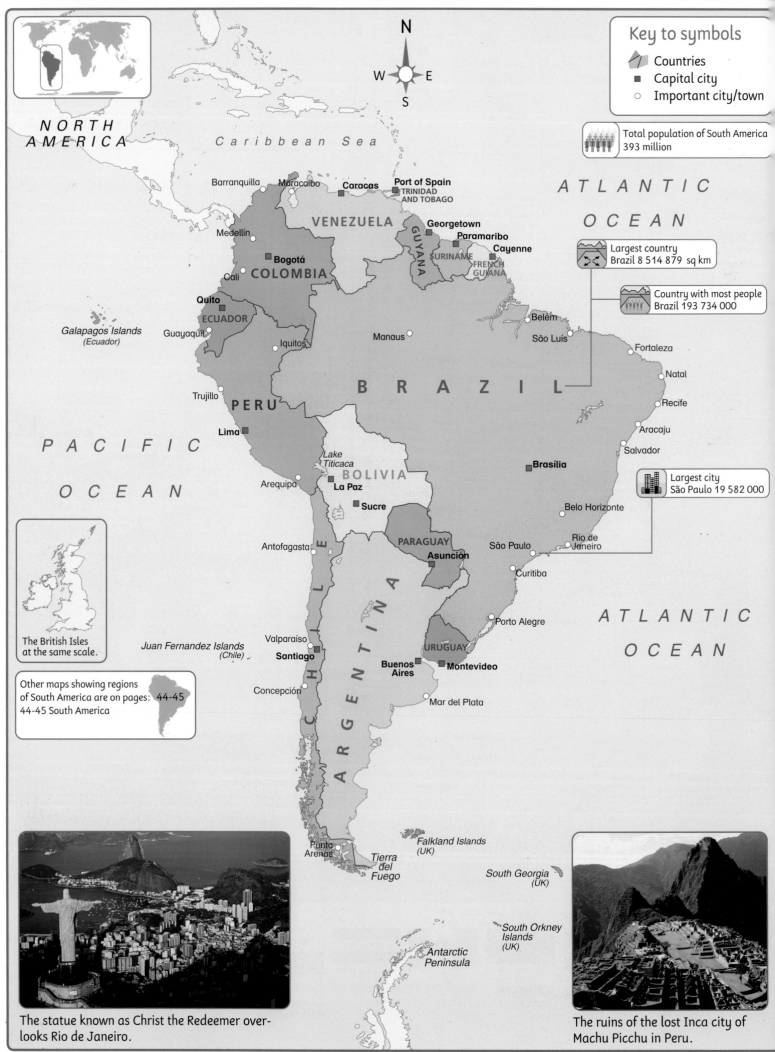

NORTH AMERICA

Caribbean Sea

N
W E
S

Key to symbols

- Countries
- Capital city
- Important city/town

Total population of South America 393 million

Largest country
Brazil 8 514 879 sq km

Country with most people
Brazil 193 734 000

Largest city
São Paulo 19 582 000

ATLANTIC OCEAN

Barranquilla
Maracaibo
Caracas
Port of Spain
TRINIDAD AND TOBAGO

VENEZUELA
Medellín
Bogotá
COLOMBIA
Cali
Quito
ECUADOR
Guayaquil

Galapagos Islands (Ecuador)

Georgetown
GUYANA
Paramaribo
SURINAME
Cayenne
FRENCH GUIANA

Belém
São Luís
Fortaleza
Natal
Recife
Aracaju
Salvador

Iquitos

Manaus

BRAZIL

Trujillo
PERU
Lima

PACIFIC OCEAN

Lake Titicaca
BOLIVIA
La Paz
Sucre
Arequipa

Brasília

Belo Horizonte

Antofagasta

PARAGUAY
Asunción

São Paulo
Rio de Janeiro

Curitiba

The British Isles at the same scale.

Juan Fernandez Islands (Chile)

Valparaíso
Santiago

Concepción

ARGENTINA
CHILE

Buenos Aires

Porto Alegre

URUGUAY
Montevideo

ATLANTIC OCEAN

Mar del Plata

Other maps showing regions of South America are on pages: 44-45
44-45 South America

Punta Arenas
Tierra del Fuego

Falkland Islands (UK)

South Georgia (UK)

South Orkney Islands (UK)

Antarctic Peninsula

The statue known as Christ the Redeemer over-looks Rio de Janeiro.

The ruins of the lost Inca city of Machu Picchu in Peru.

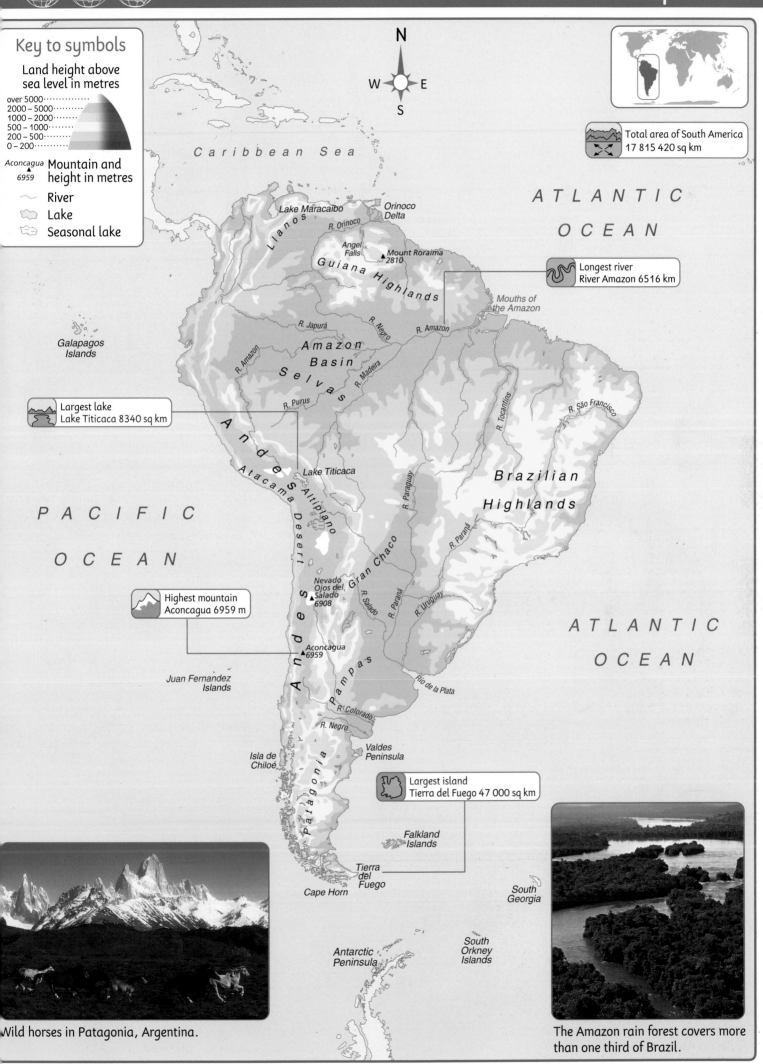

Key to symbols

Land height above sea level in metres

over 5000
2000 – 5000
1000 – 2000
500 – 1000
200 – 500
0 – 200

Aconcagua ▲ Mountain and
6959   height in metres
～ River
Lake
Seasonal lake

Total area of South America
17 815 420 sq km

Longest river
River Amazon 6516 km

Largest lake
Lake Titicaca 8340 sq km

Highest mountain
Aconcagua 6959 m

Largest island
Tierra del Fuego 47 000 sq km

Caribbean Sea

ATLANTIC OCEAN

PACIFIC OCEAN

ATLANTIC OCEAN

Lake Maracaibo
Orinoco Delta
R. Orinoco
Angel Falls
Mount Roraima 2810
Llanos
Guiana Highlands
Mouths of the Amazon
Galapagos Islands
R. Japurá
R. Negro
R. Amazon
Amazon Basin
R. Amazon
Selvas
R. Madeira
R. Purus
R. Tocantins
R. São Francisco
Andes
Atacama Desert
Altiplano
Lake Titicaca
Brazilian Highlands
Nevado Ojos del Salado 6908
Gran Chaco
R. Paraguay
R. Salado
R. Paraná
Aconcagua 6959
R. Paraná
R. Uruguay
Pampas
Juan Fernandez Islands
Rio de la Plata
R. Colorado
R. Negro
Valdes Peninsula
Isla de Chiloé
Patagonia
Falkland Islands
Tierra del Fuego
Cape Horn
South Georgia
Antarctic Peninsula
South Orkney Islands

Wild horses in Patagonia, Argentina.

The Amazon rain forest covers more than one third of Brazil.

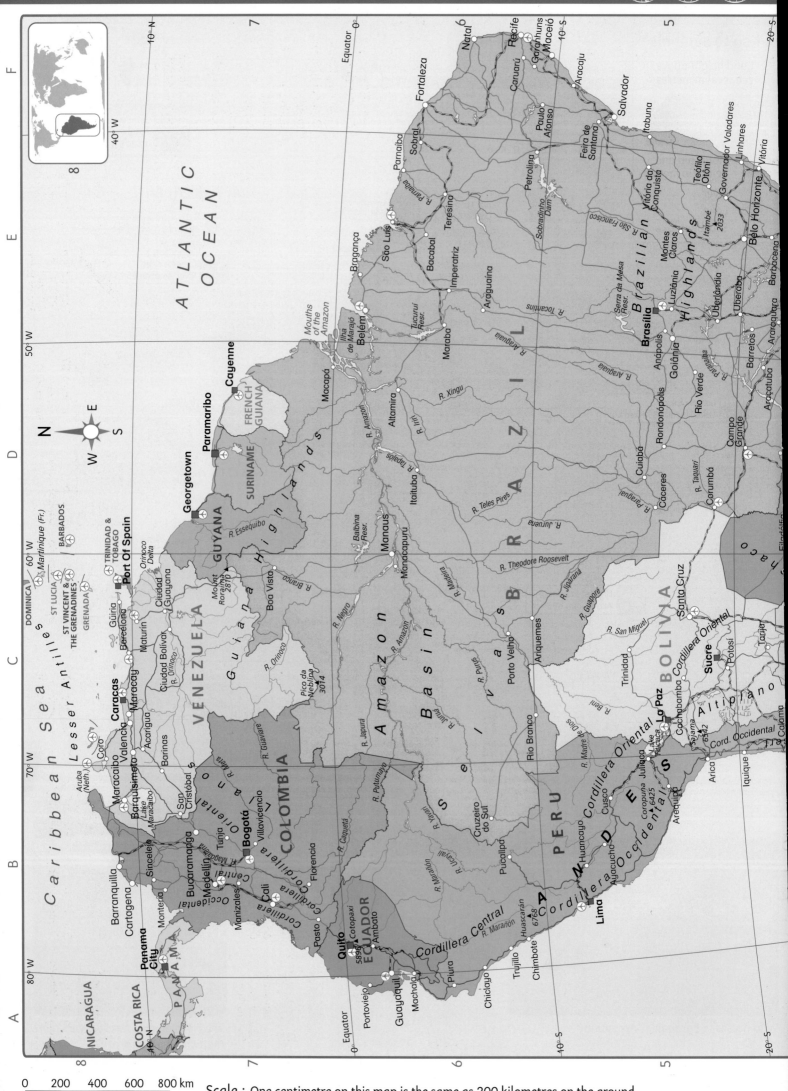

Scale : One centimetre on this map is the same as 200 kilometres on the ground.

0   200   400   600   800 km

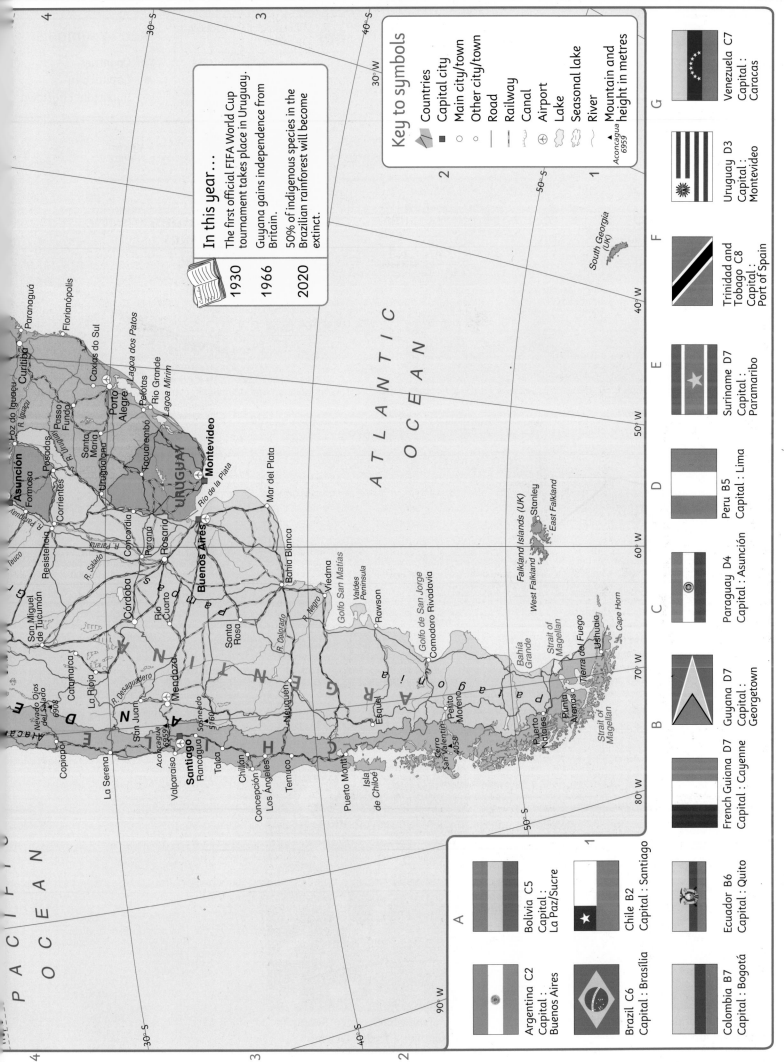

In this year...

1930	The first official FIFA World Cup tournament takes place in Uruguay.
1966	Guyana gains independence from Britain.
2020	50% of indigenous species in the Brazilian rainforest will become extinct.

Key to symbols

- Countries
- ■ Capital city
- ○ Main city/town
- ○ Other city/town
- Road
- Railway
- Canal
- ⊕ Airport
- Lake
- Seasonal lake
- River
- ▲ Mountain and height in metres
- Aconcagua 6959

A

Argentina C2
Capital :
Buenos Aires

Brazil C6
Capital : Brasília

Bolivia C5
Capital :
La Paz/Sucre

Chile B2
Capital : Santiago

Colombia B7
Capital : Bogotá

Ecuador B6
Capital : Quito

French Guiana D7
Capital : Cayenne

Guyana D7
Capital :
Georgetown

Paraguay D4
Capital : Asunción

Peru B5
Capital : Lima

Suriname D7
Capital :
Paramaribo

Trinidad and
Tobago C8
Capital :
Port of Spain

Uruguay D3
Capital :
Montevideo

Venezuela C7
Capital : Caracas

PACIFIC OCEAN

ATLANTIC OCEAN

Paranaguá
Florianópolis
Curitiba
Foz do Iguaçu
Caxias do Sul
R. Iguaçu
Lagoa dos Patos
Porto Alegre
Pelotas
Rio Grande
Lagoa Mirim
Posso Fundo
Santa Maria
Tacuarembó
Uruguaiana
R. Uruguai
Posadas
Santa Fé
URUGUAY
Montevideo
Asunción
Formosa
Corrientes
Resistencia
R. Paraguai
R. Teuco
Concordia
Paraná
Rosario
Buenos Aires
Río de la Plata
Mar del Plata
R. Paraná
R. Salado
San Miguel
de Tucumán
Córdoba
Río Cuarto
Bahía Blanca
Catamarca
La Rioja
R. Desaguadero
Santa Rosa
Viedma
R. Negro
Golfo San Matías
Valdés Peninsula
Rawson
Nevado Ojos
del Salado
6900
San Juan
Mendoza
Aconcagua
6959
San Rafael
Neuquén
R. Colorado
ARGENTINA
Golfo de San Jorge
Comodoro Rivadavia
Copiapó
Antofagasta
La Serena
Valparaíso
Santiago
Rancagua
5760
Talca
Chillán
Concepción
Los Ángeles
Temuco
Puerto Montt
Isla
de Chiloé
Cerro
San Valentín
4058
Esquel
Perito
Moreno
Patagonia
Puerto
Natales
Punta
Arenas
Strait of
Magellan
Bahía Grande
Strait of
Magellan
Tierra del Fuego
Ushuaia
Cape Horn
Falkland Islands (UK)
West Falkland
East Falkland
Stanley
South Georgia (UK)

90°W 80°W 70°W 60°W 50°W 40°W 30°W

30°S 40°S 50°S

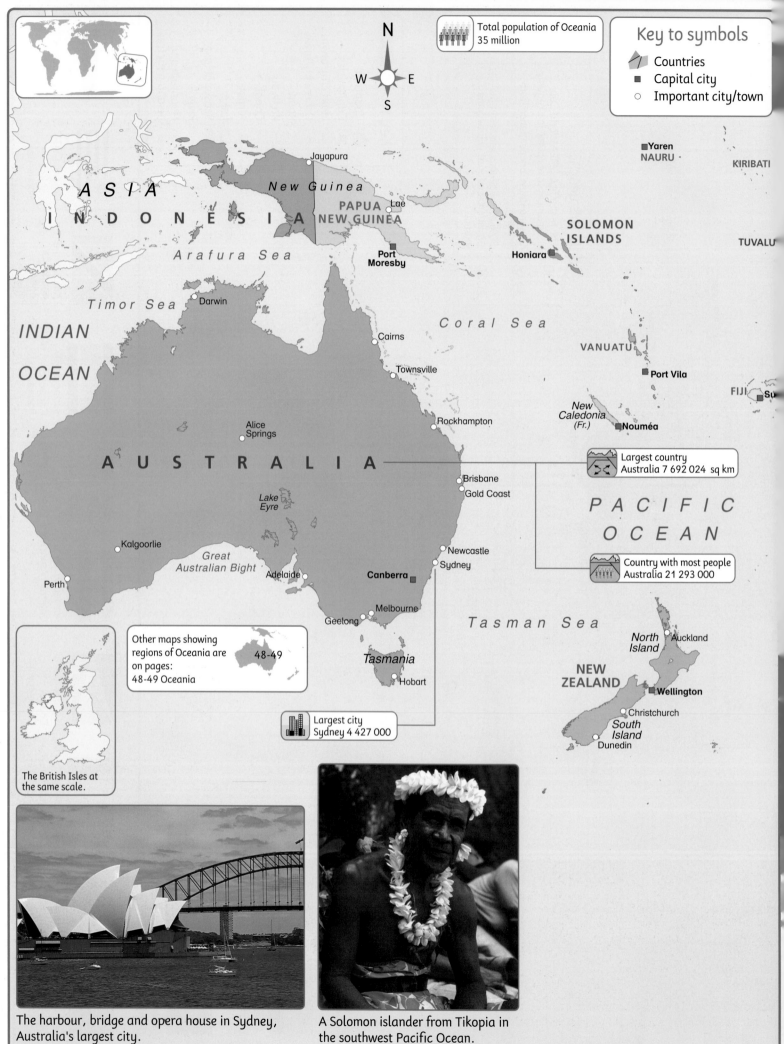

Total population of Oceania
35 million

Key to symbols
- ◢ Countries
- ■ Capital city
- ○ Important city/town

N
W E
S

Yaren
NAURU
KIRIBATI

ASIA
INDONESIA

New Guinea
Jayapura

PAPUA
NEW GUINEA
Lae

Arafura Sea

Port
Moresby

SOLOMON
ISLANDS

TUVALU

Honiara

Timor Sea
Darwin

Coral Sea

INDIAN

OCEAN

Cairns

Townsville

VANUATU

Port Vila

FIJI Su

New
Caledonia
(Fr.)
Nouméa

Alice
Springs

Rockhampton

AUSTRALIA

Largest country
Australia 7 692 024 sq km

PACIFIC

OCEAN

Brisbane
Gold Coast

Lake
Eyre

Country with most people
Australia 21 293 000

Kalgoorlie

Great
Australian Bight

Newcastle

Adelaide

Sydney

Perth

Canberra

Melbourne
Geelong

Tasman Sea

North
Island
Auckland

Other maps showing
regions of Oceania are
on pages:
48-49
48-49 Oceania

Tasmania

NEW
ZEALAND

Wellington

Hobart

Christchurch

South
Island
Dunedin

The British Isles at
the same scale.

Largest city
Sydney 4 427 000

The harbour, bridge and opera house in Sydney,
Australia's largest city.

A Solomon islander from Tikopia in
the southwest Pacific Ocean.

Scale : One centimetre on this map is the same as 325 kilometres on the ground.

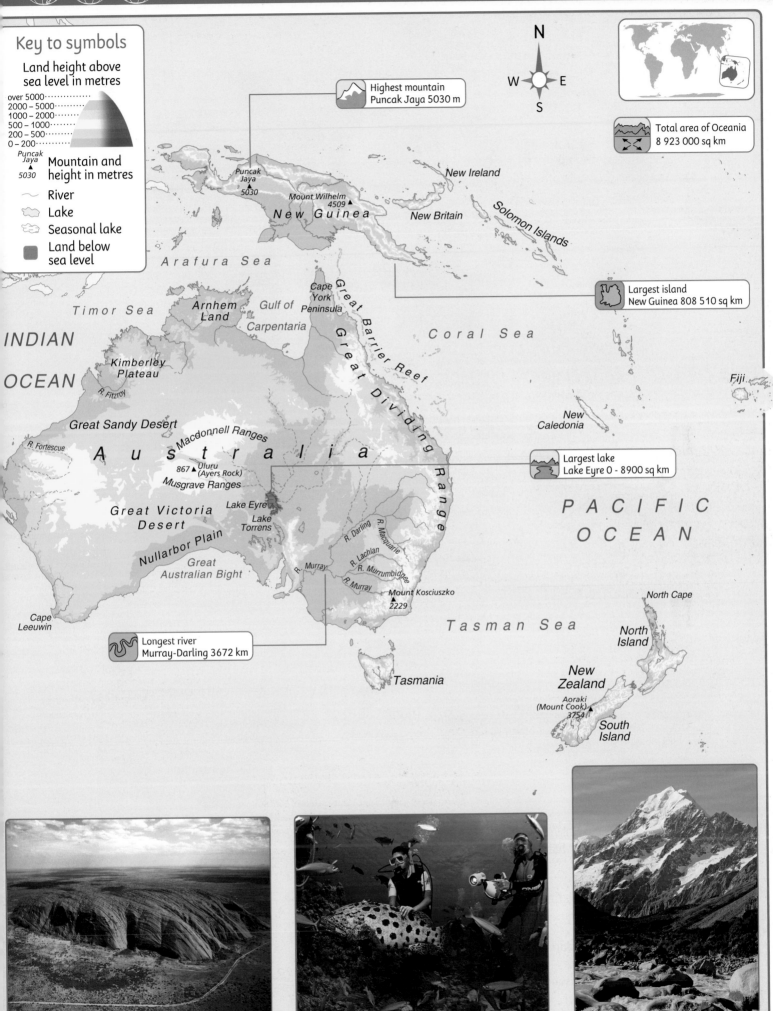

Key to symbols

Land height above sea level in metres

over 5000
2000 – 5000
1000 – 2000
500 – 1000
200 – 500
0 – 200

Puncak Jaya 5030 ▲ Mountain and height in metres

⌒ River
Lake
Seasonal lake
Land below sea level

Highest mountain
Puncak Jaya 5030 m

N W E S

Total area of Oceania
8 923 000 sq km

Largest island
New Guinea 808 510 sq km

Largest lake
Lake Eyre 0 - 8900 sq km

Longest river
Murray-Darling 3672 km

Puncak Jaya 5030

New Guinea

New Ireland

Mount Wilhelm 4509 ▲

New Britain

Solomon Islands

Arafura Sea

Cape York Peninsula

Gulf of Carpentaria

Great Barrier Reef

Coral Sea

Fiji

Timor Sea

Arnhem Land

INDIAN OCEAN

Kimberley Plateau

R. Fitzroy

Great Sandy Desert

R. Fortescue

Australia

Macdonnell Ranges

867 ▲ Uluru (Ayers Rock)
Musgrave Ranges

Great Victoria Desert

Lake Eyre
Lake Torrens

Nullarbor Plain

Great Australian Bight

R. Murray

R. Darling
R. Macquarie
R. Lachlan
R. Murrumbidgee
R. Murray

Great Dividing Range

New Caledonia

PACIFIC OCEAN

Cape Leeuwin

Mount Kosciuszko 2229 ▲

Tasman Sea

Tasmania

North Cape

North Island

New Zealand

Aoraki (Mount Cook) 3754 ▲

South Island

Uluru (Ayers Rock), a large single rock outcrop in Australia.

Divers feed fish on the Great Barrier Reef, Australia.

Aoraki (Mount Cook), the highest mountain in New Zealand.

Key to symbols

Countries
Capital city
Main city/town
Other city/town
Road
Railway
Puncak Jaya 5030

Airport
Lake
Seasonal lake
River
Mountain and height in metres

Scale : One centimetre on this map is the same as 200 kilometres on the ground.

0 200 400 600 800 km

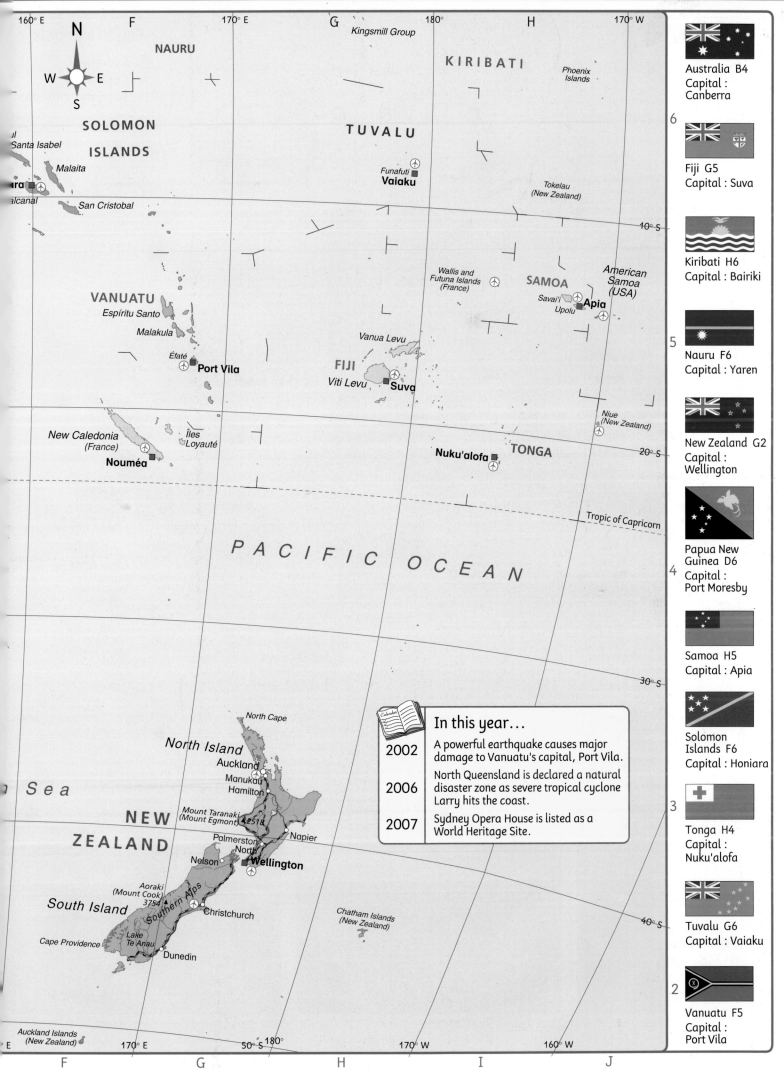

N
W E
S

160° E

NAURU

SOLOMON
ISLANDS

Santa Isabel

Malaita

ra

lcanal

San Cristobal

170° E

G

Kingsmill Group

KIRIBATI

180°

H

Phoenix
Islands

170° W

TUVALU

Funafuti
Vaiaku

Tokelau
(New Zealand)

10° S

VANUATU

Espíritu Santo

Malakula

Éfaté
Port Vila

New Caledonia
(France)

Îles
Loyauté

Nouméa

Vanua Levu

FIJI

Viti Levu

Suva

Wallis and
Futuna Islands
(France)

SAMOA

Savai'i
Upolu

American
Samoa
(USA)

Apia

Niue
(New Zealand)

TONGA

Nuku'alofa

20° S

Tropic of Capricorn

P A C I F I C   O C E A N

30° S

Sea

NEW

ZEALAND

North Cape

North Island

Auckland

Manukau

Hamilton

Mount Taranaki
(Mount Egmont) 2518

Palmerston
North

Napier

Nelson

Wellington

Aoraki
(Mount Cook)

Southern Alps

South Island

3754

Christchurch

Cape Providence

Lake
Te Anau

Dunedin

Auckland Islands
(New Zealand)

170° E

180°

50° S

170° W

40° S

160° W

F

G

H

I

J

Chatham Islands
(New Zealand)

In this year…

2002 A powerful earthquake causes major damage to Vanuatu's capital, Port Vila.

2006 North Queensland is declared a natural disaster zone as severe tropical cyclone Larry hits the coast.

2007 Sydney Opera House is listed as a World Heritage Site.

Australia B4
Capital : Canberra

Fiji G5
Capital : Suva

Kiribati H6
Capital : Bairiki

Nauru F6
Capital : Yaren

New Zealand G2
Capital : Wellington

Papua New Guinea D6
Capital : Port Moresby

Samoa H5
Capital : Apia

Solomon Islands F6
Capital : Honiara

Tonga H4
Capital : Nuku'alofa

Tuvalu G6
Capital : Vaiaku

Vanuatu F5
Capital : Port Vila

6

5

4

3

2

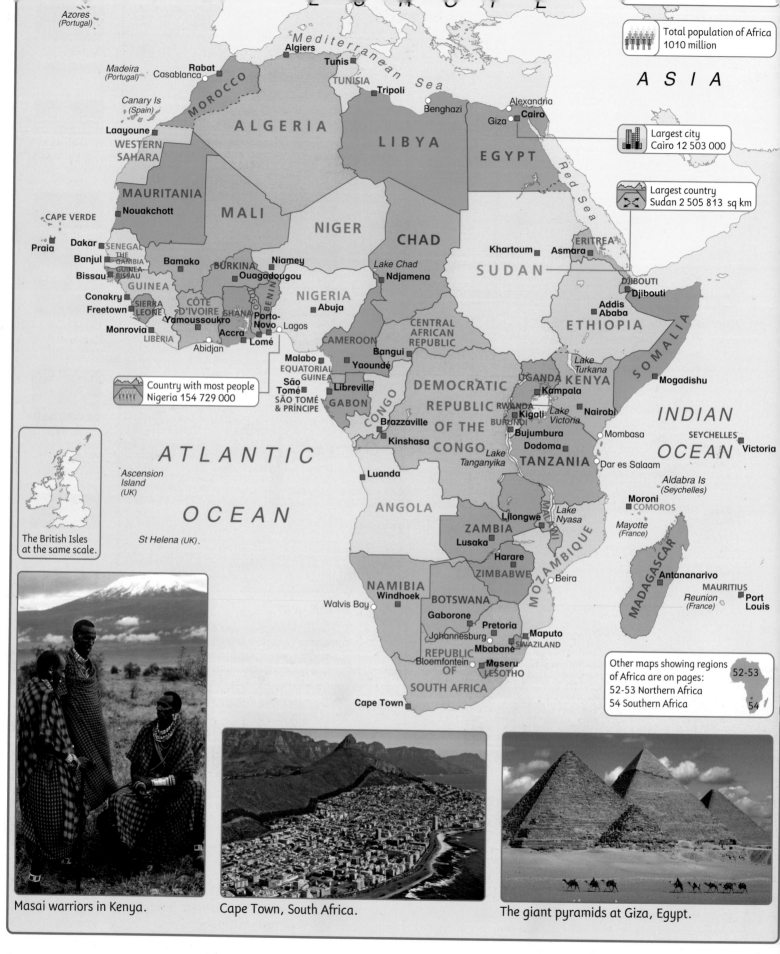

Azores
(Portugal)

E U R O P E

Mediterranean Sea

Algiers

Tunis
TUNISIA

Tripoli

Benghazi

Alexandria
Giza Cairo

ASIA

Total population of Africa
1010 million

Madeira
(Portugal) Casablanca Rabat

MOROCCO

Canary Is
(Spain)

Laayoune

WESTERN
SAHARA

A L G E R I A

L I B Y A

E G Y P T

Red Sea

Largest city
Cairo 12 503 000

CAPE VERDE

Praia

Dakar

Banjul

Bissau

MAURITANIA

Nouakchott

M A L I

N I G E R

C H A D

Lake Chad

Ndjamena

Khartoum Asmara
ERITREA

S U D A N

DJIBOUTI
Djibouti

Largest country
Sudan 2 505 813 sq km

SENEGAL
THE
GAMBIA
GUINEA-
BISSAU

GUINEA

Bamako

BURKINA

Niamey

Ouagadougou

N I G E R I A

Abuja

Addis
Ababa

E T H I O P I A

Conakry
Freetown

SIERRA
LEONE

CÔTE
D'IVOIRE
GHANA

Yamoussoukro

Monrovia

LIBERIA

Accra

Abidjan

Porto-
Novo

Lomé

Lagos

BENIN

CENTRAL
AFRICAN
REPUBLIC

Lake
Turkana

UGANDA KENYA

S O M A L I A

Mogadishu

Country with most people
Nigeria 154 729 000

Malabo

EQUATORIAL
GUINEA

São
Tomé

SÃO TOMÉ
& PRÍNCIPE

CAMEROON

Yaoundé

Bangui

Libreville

GABON

CONGO

DEMOCRATIC

REPUBLIC

OF THE

CONGO

Brazzaville

Kinshasa

Kampala

RWANDA

Kigali

BURUNDI

Bujumbura

Dodoma

Lake
Victoria

Nairobi

Mombasa

INDIAN

OCEAN

SEYCHELLES

Victoria

Lake
Tanganyika

TANZANIA

Dar es Salaam

ATLANTIC

Ascension
Island
(UK)

OCEAN

St Helena (UK)

Luanda

ANGOLA

Lake
Nyasa

Lilongwe

Aldabra Is
(Seychelles)

Moroni
COMOROS

Mayotte
(France)

The British Isles
at the same scale.

ZAMBIA

Lusaka

Harare

ZIMBABWE

MALAWI

MOZAMBIQUE

Beira

MADAGASCAR

Antananarivo

MAURITIUS

Reunion
(France)

Port
Louis

NAMIBIA

Windhoek

Walvis Bay

BOTSWANA

Gaborone

Johannesburg

Pretoria

Mbabane

SWAZILAND

Maputo

Bloemfontein

REPUBLIC
OF

Maseru
LESOTHO

Other maps showing regions
of Africa are on pages:
52-53 Northern Africa
54 Southern Africa

52-53

54

SOUTH AFRICA

Cape Town

Masai warriors in Kenya.

Cape Town, South Africa.

The giant pyramids at Giza, Egypt.

0   450   900   1350   1800   2250 km

Scale : One centimetre on this map is the same as 450 kilometres on the ground.

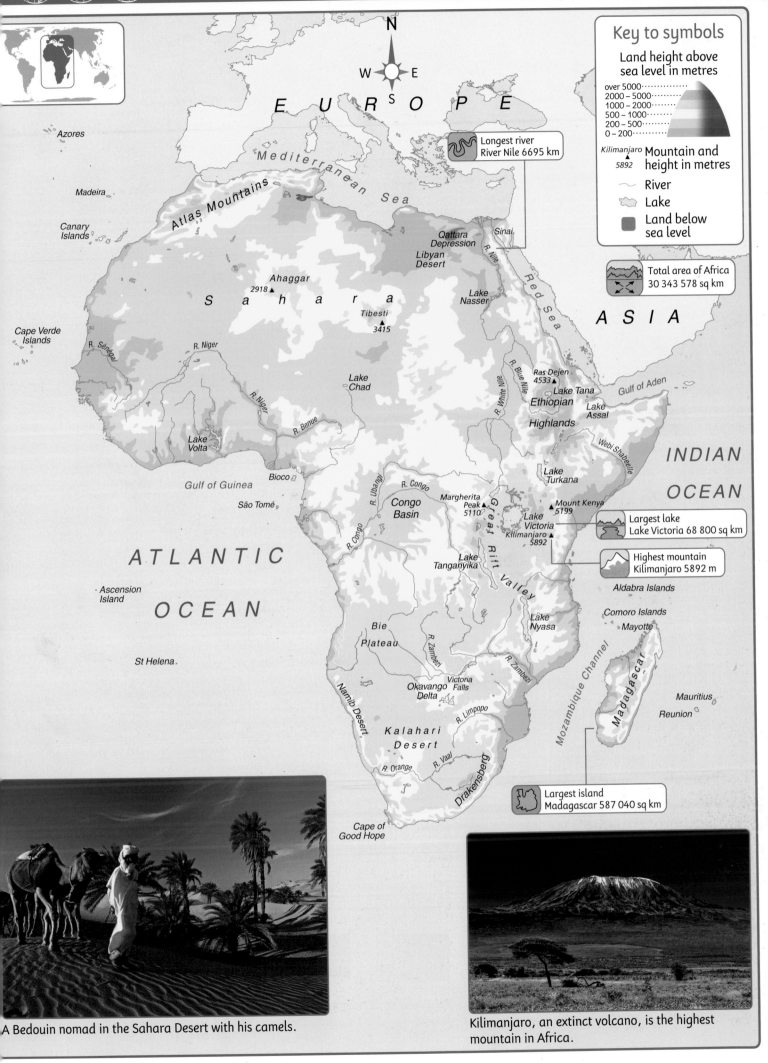

Key to symbols
Land height above
sea level in metres
over 5000
2000 – 5000
1000 – 2000
500 – 1000
200 – 500
0 – 200
Kilimanjaro ▲ Mountain and
5892 height in metres
～ River
Lake
Land below
sea level

N
W E
S

E U R O P E

Azores

Madeira

*Canary
Islands*

*Cape Verde
Islands*

Mediterranean Sea

Atlas Mountains

S a h a r a

Ahaggar
2918 ▲

Tibesti
3415 ▲

*Qattara
Depression*

*Libyan
Desert*

Sinai

Longest river
River Nile 6695 km

R. Nile

*Lake
Nasser*

Red Sea

A S I A

Total area of Africa
30 343 578 sq km

R. Sénégal

R. Niger

R. Niger

R. Benue

Lake
Chad

R. White Nile

R. Blue Nile

*Ras Dejen
4533* ▲

Lake Tana

*Ethiopian
Highlands*

*Lake
Assal*

Gulf of Aden

Webi Shabeelle

*Lake
Volta*

Gulf of Guinea

Bioco

São Tomé

R. Ubangi

R. Congo

R. Congo

R. Congo

Congo
Basin

*Margherita
Peak* ▲
5110

Great Rift Valley

*Lake
Turkana*

INDIAN

OCEAN

*Mount Kenya
5199* ▲

Lake
Victoria

*Kilimanjaro
5892* ▲

Largest lake
Lake Victoria 68 800 sq km

Highest mountain
Kilimanjaro 5892 m

Aldabra Islands

A T L A N T I C

O C E A N

*Ascension
Island*

St Helena

*Lake
Tanganyika*

*Bie
Plateau*

R. Zambezi

*Okavango
Delta*

*Victoria
Falls*

R. Zambezi

*Lake
Nyasa*

Comoro Islands

Mayotte

Mozambique Channel

Madagascar

Mauritius

Reunion

Namib Desert

K a l a h a r i
D e s e r t

R. Orange

R. Vaal

R. Limpopo

Drakensberg

Largest island
Madagascar 587 040 sq km

*Cape of
Good Hope*

A Bedouin nomad in the Sahara Desert with his camels.

Kilimanjaro, an extinct volcano, is the highest
mountain in Africa.

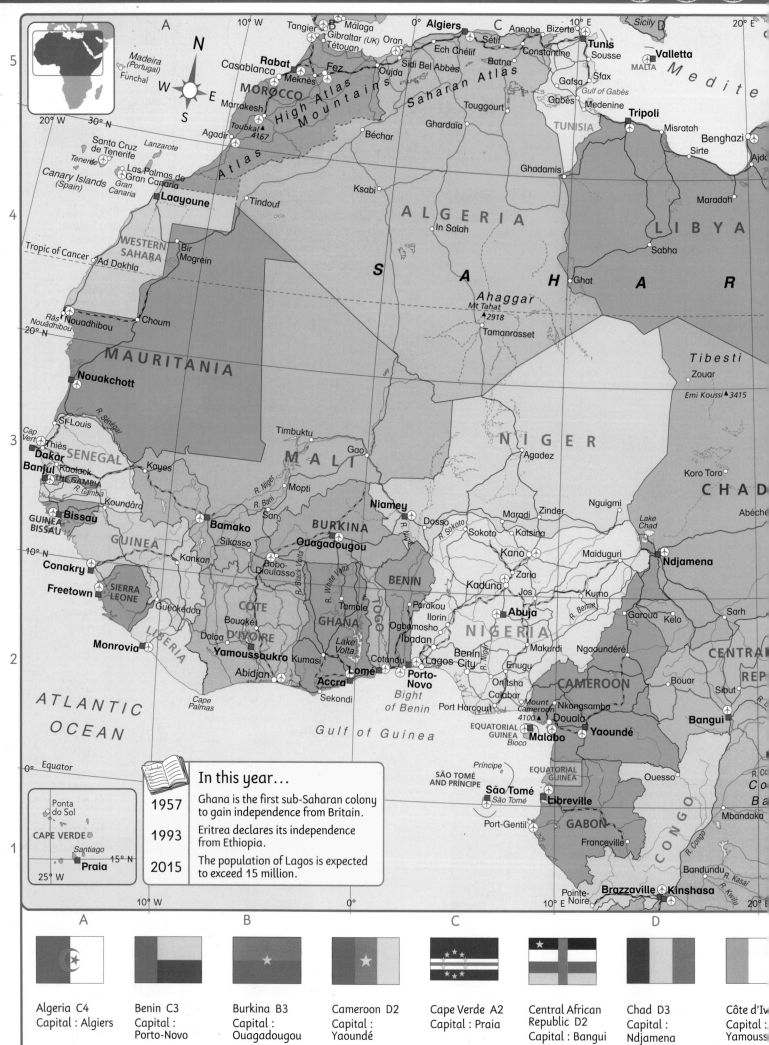

In this year...

1957	Ghana is the first sub-Saharan colony to gain independence from Britain.
1993	Eritrea declares its independence from Ethiopia.
2015	The population of Lagos is expected to exceed 15 million.

Algeria C4
Capital : Algiers

Benin C3
Capital : Porto-Novo

Burkina B3
Capital : Ouagadougou

Cameroon D2
Capital : Yaoundé

Cape Verde A2
Capital : Praia

Central African Republic D2
Capital : Bangui

Chad D3
Capital : Ndjamena

Côte d'Iv
Capital : Yamouss

0 200 400 600 800 km

Scale : One centimetre on this map is the same as 200 kilometres on the ground.

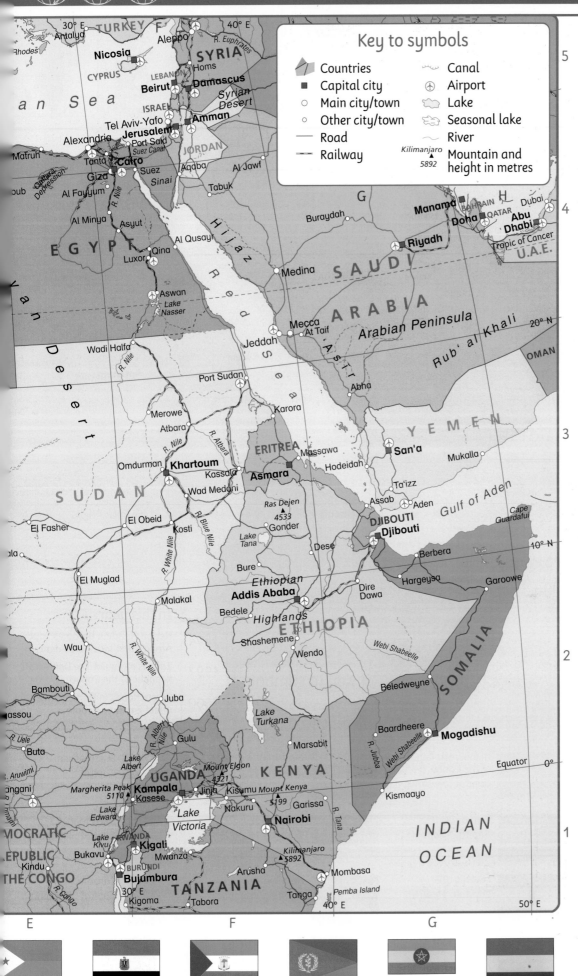

Key to symbols

| Countries |
| Capital city |
| ○ Main city/town |
| ○ Other city/town |
| — Road |
| Railway |

| Canal |
| Airport |
| Lake |
| Seasonal lake |
| River |
| Kilimanjaro 5892 ▲ Mountain and height in metres |

The Gambia A3
Capital : Banjul

Nigeria C2
Capital : Abuja

Ghana B2
Capital : Accra

São Tomé and Príncipe C2
Capital : São Tomé

Guinea A3
Capital : Conakry

Senegal A3
Capital : Dakar

Guinea-Bissau A3
Capital : Bissau

Sierra Leone A2
Capital : Freetown

Liberia A2
Capital : Monrovia

Somalia G2
Capital : Mogadishu

Libya D4
Capital : Tripoli

Sudan E3
Capital : Khartoum

Mali B3
Capital : Bamako

Togo C2
Capital : Lomé

Mauritania A3
Capital : Nouakchott

Tunisia C5
Capital : Tunis

Morocco B5
Capital : Rabat

Uganda F2
Capital : Kampala

Djibouti G3
Capital : Djibouti

Egypt E4
Capital : Cairo

Equatorial Guinea C2
Capital : Malabo

Eritrea F3
Capital : Asmara

Ethiopia F2
Capital : Addis Ababa

Gabon D1
Capital : Libreville

Niger C3
Capital : Niamey

Western Sahara A4
Capital : Laayoune

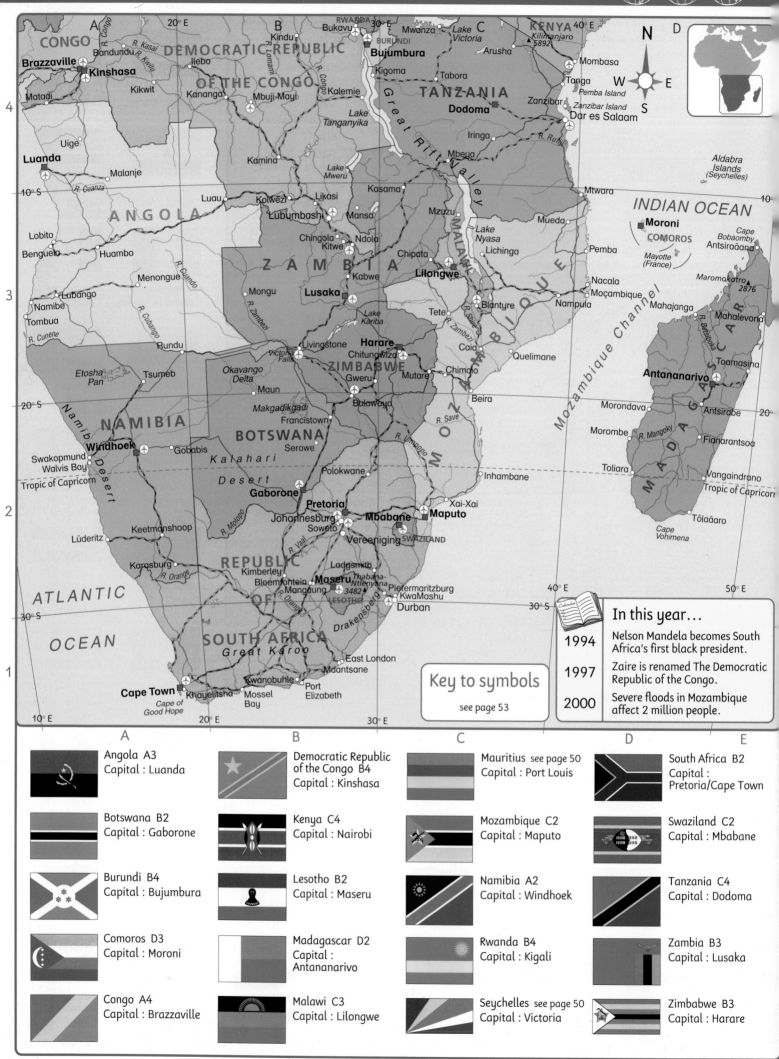

Key to symbols

see page 53

In this year...

1994 — Nelson Mandela becomes South Africa's first black president.

1997 — Zaire is renamed The Democratic Republic of the Congo.

2000 — Severe floods in Mozambique affect 2 million people.

Angola A3
Capital : Luanda

Democratic Republic of the Congo B4
Capital : Kinshasa

Mauritius see page 50
Capital : Port Louis

South Africa B2
Capital : Pretoria/Cape Town

Botswana B2
Capital : Gaborone

Kenya C4
Capital : Nairobi

Mozambique C2
Capital : Maputo

Swaziland C2
Capital : Mbabane

Burundi B4
Capital : Bujumbura

Lesotho B2
Capital : Maseru

Namibia A2
Capital : Windhoek

Tanzania C4
Capital : Dodoma

Comoros D3
Capital : Moroni

Madagascar D2
Capital : Antananarivo

Rwanda B4
Capital : Kigali

Zambia B3
Capital : Lusaka

Congo A4
Capital : Brazzaville

Malawi C3
Capital : Lilongwe

Seychelles see page 50
Capital : Victoria

Zimbabwe B3
Capital : Harare

Scale : One centimetre on this map is the same as 200 kilometres on the ground.

0 200 400 600 800 km

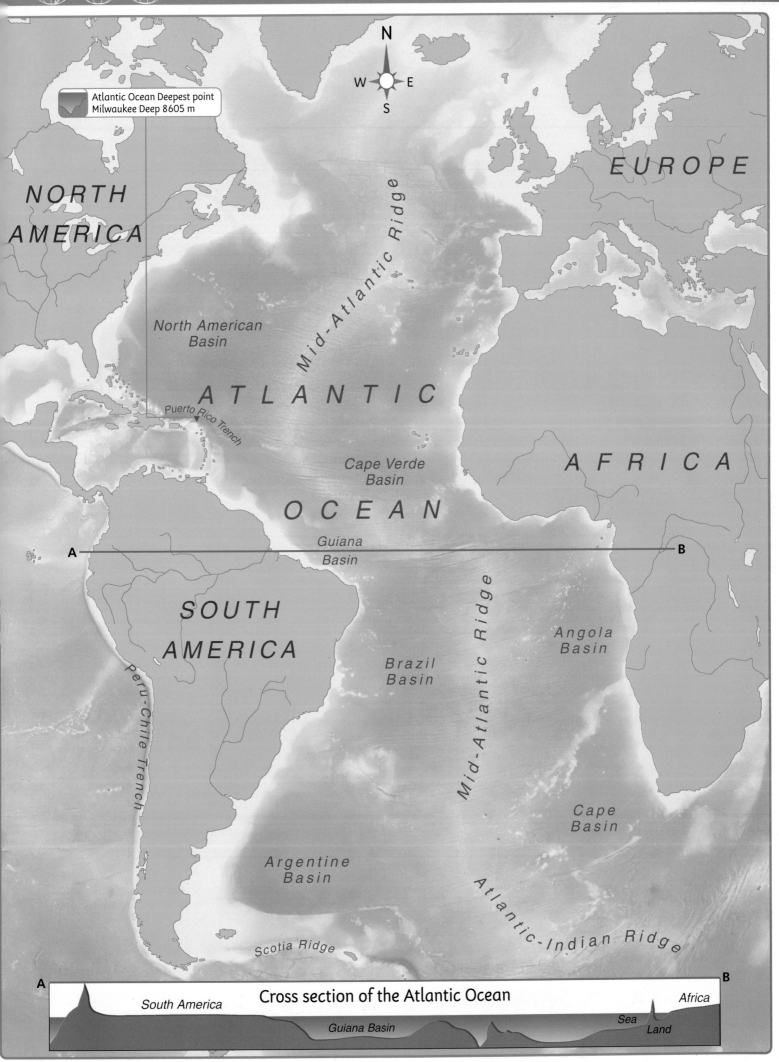

Atlantic Ocean Deepest point
Milwaukee Deep 8605 m

N
W E
S

NORTH
AMERICA

EUROPE

North American
Basin

Mid-Atlantic Ridge

A T L A N T I C

Puerto Rico Trench

Cape Verde
Basin

AFRICA

O C E A N

Guiana
Basin

A   B

SOUTH
AMERICA

Brazil
Basin

Angola
Basin

Mid-Atlantic Ridge

Peru-Chile Trench

Cape
Basin

Argentine
Basin

Atlantic-Indian Ridge

Scotia Ridge

A   B

Cross section of the Atlantic Ocean

South America   Africa

Sea
Land

Guiana Basin

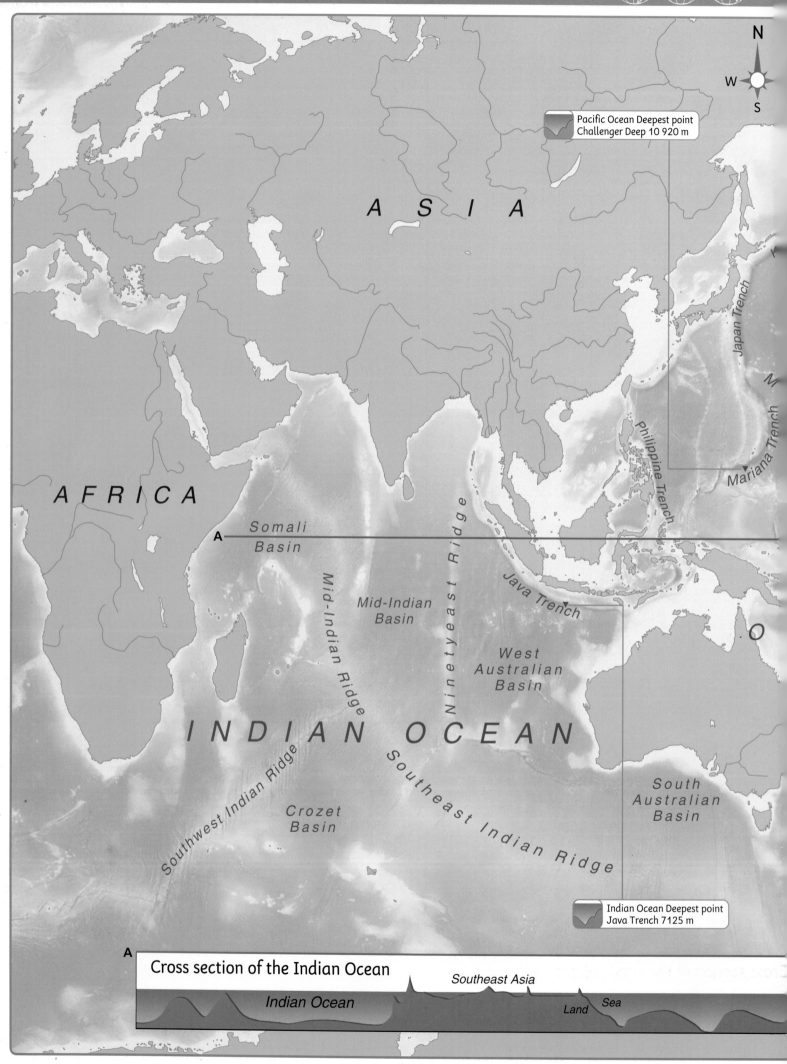

N
W   S

Pacific Ocean Deepest point
Challenger Deep 10 920 m

A S I A

Japan Trench

Mariana Trench

Philippine Trench

AFRICA

A   Somali
Basin

Mid-Indian Ridge

Mid-Indian
Basin

Ninetyeast Ridge

Java Trench

West
Australian
Basin

O

INDIAN   OCEAN

Southwest Indian Ridge

Crozet
Basin

Southeast Indian Ridge

South
Australian
Basin

Indian Ocean Deepest point
Java Trench 7125 m

A

Cross section of the Indian Ocean

Southeast Asia

Indian Ocean

Land   Sea

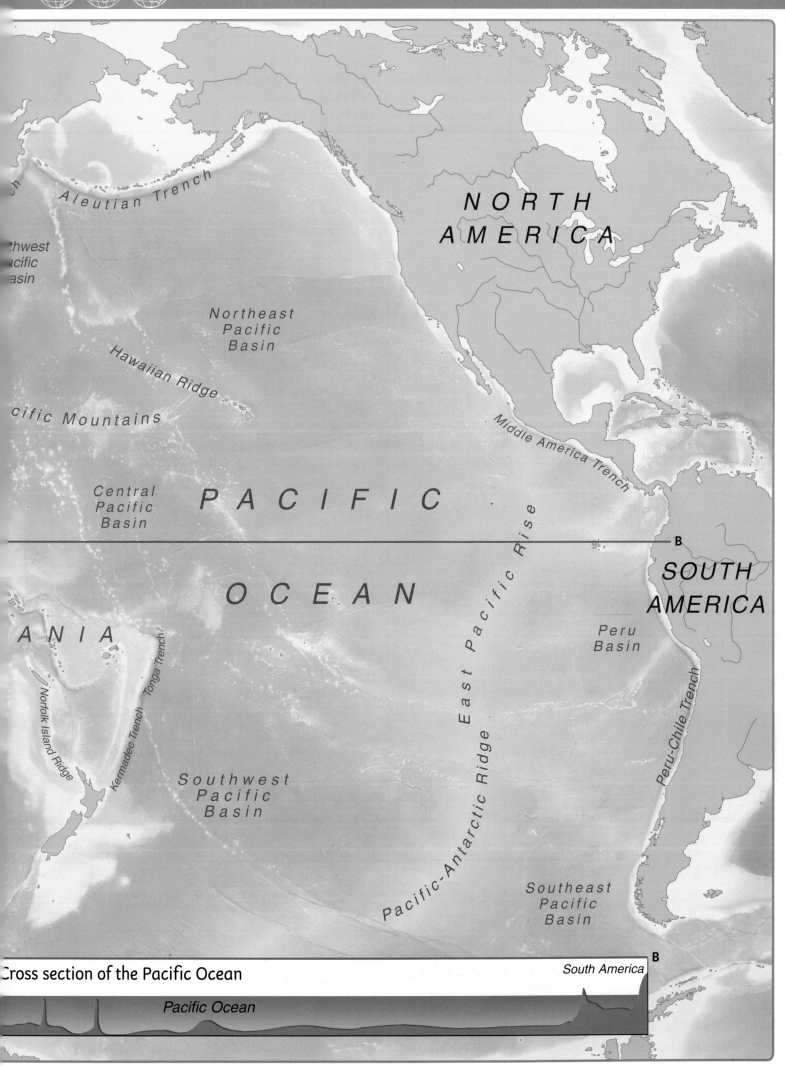

Aleutian Trench

…thwest …cific …asin

NORTH AMERICA

Northeast Pacific Basin

Hawaiian Ridge

…cific Mountains

Central Pacific Basin

PACIFIC

Middle America Trench

East Pacific Rise

B

SOUTH AMERICA

OCEAN

…ANIA

Norfolk Island Ridge

Kermadec Trench

Tonga Trench

Southwest Pacific Basin

Peru Basin

Peru-Chile Trench

Pacific-Antarctic Ridge

Southeast Pacific Basin

Cross section of the Pacific Ocean

B

South America

Pacific Ocean

Key to symbols

Land height above sea level in metres

- over 2000
- 1000 – 2000
- 500 – 1000
- 200 – 500
- 0 – 200

- ~ River
- Lake
- Ice cap
- Polar pack ice
- Drifting ice

In this year...

- **1969** The first surface crossing of the Arctic Ocean is completed.
- **2007** Area of Arctic ice falls to record low of 5.2 million sq km.
- **2007** A Russian expedition makes the first ever manned descent to the bottom of the ocean at the North Pole.

The British Isles at the same scale.

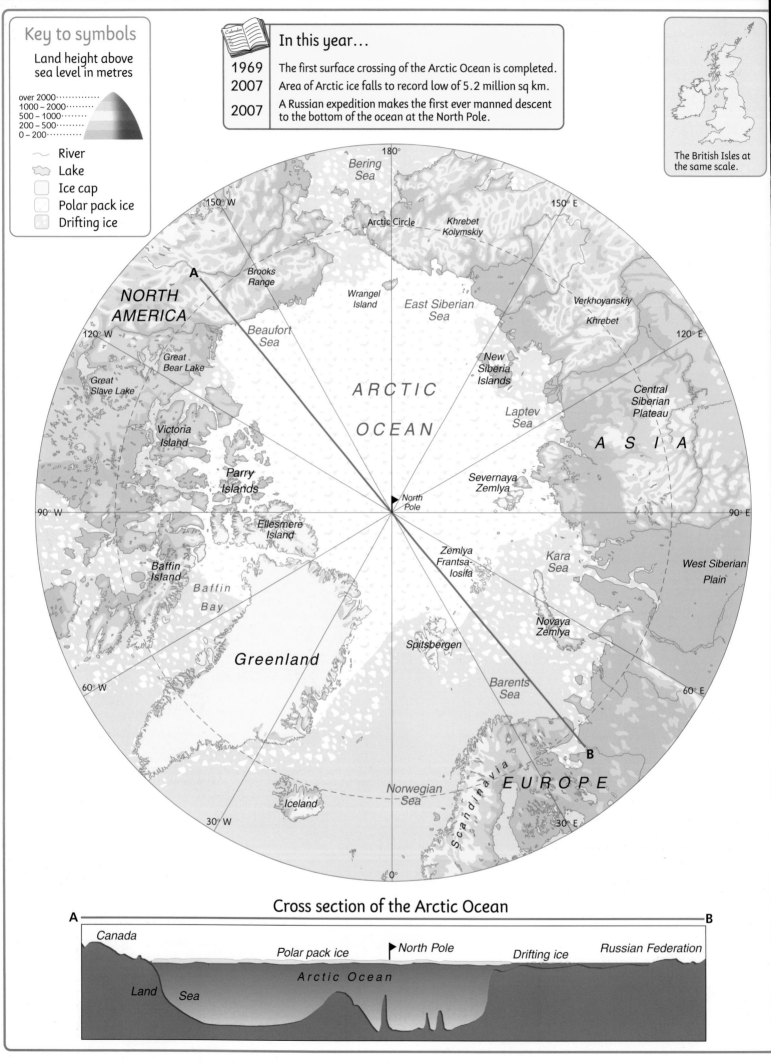

180°

Bering Sea

150° W

Arctic Circle

Khrebet Kolymskiy

150° E

A

Brooks Range

Wrangel Island

East Siberian Sea

Verkhoyanskiy

NORTH AMERICA

120° W

Beaufort Sea

120° E

Khrebet

Great Bear Lake

New Siberia Islands

Central Siberian Plateau

Great Slave Lake

A R C T I C

Laptev Sea

A S I A

Victoria Island

O C E A N

Parry Islands

Severnaya Zemlya

90° W

North Pole

90° E

Ellesmere Island

Zemlya Frantsa-Iosifa

Kara Sea

West Siberian Plain

Baffin Island

Baffin Bay

Novaya Zemlya

60° W

Greenland

Spitsbergen

Barents Sea

B

60° E

30° W

Iceland

Norwegian Sea

Scandinavia

E U R O P E

30° E

0°

Cross section of the Arctic Ocean

A ——————————————————— **B**

Canada

Polar pack ice

▶ North Pole

Drifting ice

Russian Federation

Land   Sea

Arctic Ocean

| 0 | 500 | 1000 | 1500 | 2000 km |

Scale : One centimetre on this map is the same as 350 kilometres on the ground.

Manned bases in the Antarctic Peninsula

① Comandante Ferraz (Brazil)
② King Sejong (Korea)
③ Artigas (Uruguay)
④ Frei (Chile)
⑤ Bellingshausen (Russian Federation)
⑥ Great Wall (China)
⑦ Escudero (Chile)
⑧ Jubany (Argentina)
⑨ Arctowski (Poland)
⑩ O'Higgins (Chile)
⑪ San Martin (Argentina)

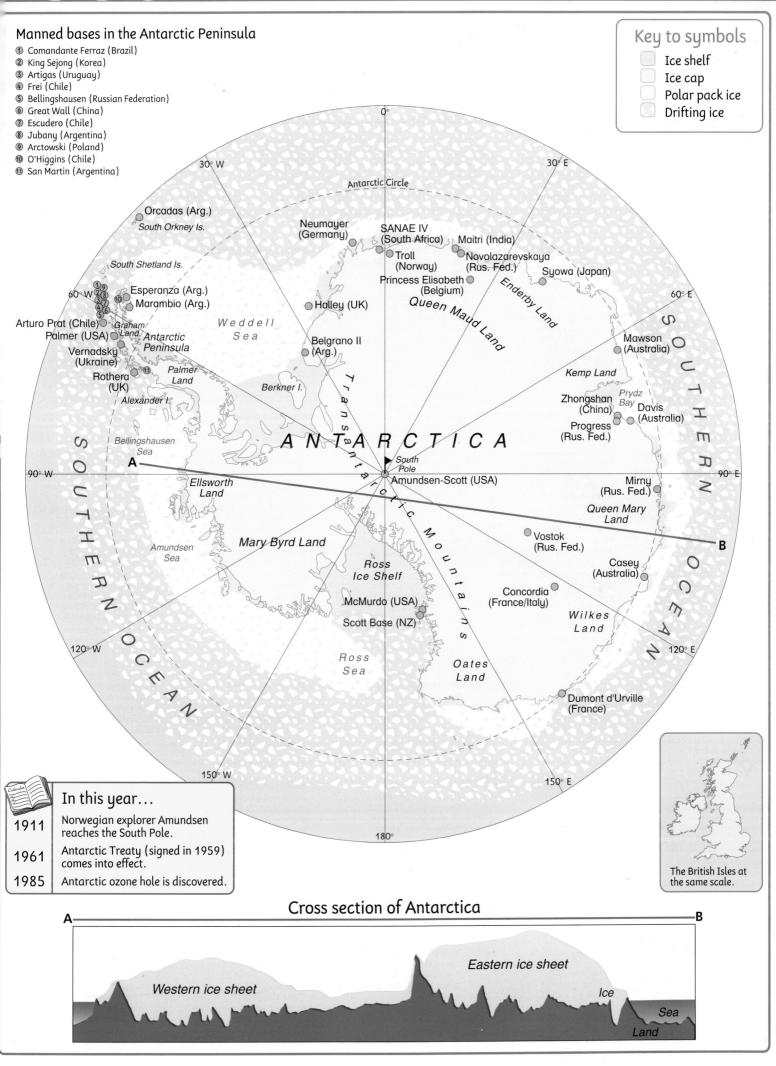

Key to symbols

Ice shelf
Ice cap
Polar pack ice
Drifting ice

The British Isles at the same scale.

In this year...

1911 Norwegian explorer Amundsen reaches the South Pole.

1961 Antarctic Treaty (signed in 1959) comes into effect.

1985 Antarctic ozone hole is discovered.

Cross section of Antarctica

Western ice sheet

Eastern ice sheet

Ice

Sea

Land

0   500   1000   1500   2000 km

Scale : One centimetre on this map is the same as 350 kilometres on the ground.

place name — grid code
Cairo *capital* 53 F5
page number
cities and towns are shown in green

place name — grid code
Tyne *river* 18 D4
page number
water features are shown in blue

place name — grid code
Italy *country* 24 G3
page number
countries and states are shown in red

place name — grid code
Corsica *island* 24 F3
page number
physical features are shown in black

Photo credits

Science Photo Library:
p15 London, p16 UK Satellite image, p17 Beachy Head

Mark Steward:
p17 Glen Coe, p26 Kuala Lumpur, p35 Grand Canyon, p46 Sydney

Corbis:
p34 Times Square, Jose Fuste Raga, p42 Rio de Janeiro, Richard T. Nowitz

Still Pictures:
p13 Etna eruption, Otto Hahn, p14 Brussels, Wim Van Cappellen, p26 Shanghai, Markus Dlouhy, p43 Argentina, Galen Rowell, p43 Rainforest, Jacques Jangoux, p46 Solomon islander, K. Hympendahl, p47 Great Barrier Reef, Fred Bavendam, p47 Uluru, Raimund Franken, p50 Masai warriors, Friedrich Stark, p51 Sahara Desert, Frans Lemmens

Shutterstock:
p12 Colosseum, SF photo, p12 Eiffel Tower, Igor Rivilis, p13 Norway, Plotnikoff, p27 Rice paddies, Bali, Lim Yong Hian, p27 Mount Everest, Pichugin Dmitry, p34 Washington, Jonathan Larsen, p35 Niagara Falls, Howard Sandler, p42 Machu Picchu, Amy Nicole Harris, p47 Aoraki (Mount Cook), Sander van Sinttruye, p50 Cape Town, W. Woyke, p50 Giza, sculpies, p51 Kilimanjaro, enote

Acknowledgement

Editorial Adviser: Professor Simon Catling, pp2-7

Maps on the pages listed below are derived in part from material originally published in Collins Longman Atlases:
Keystart Junior Atlas: Pp8-9, p12, pp22-23, pp24-25, p26, p34, p42, p46, p50. Foundation Atlas: Pp58, p59